PRISON SECRETS

THE UNTOLD TRUTHS ABOUT ONE OF AMERICAS NOTORIOUS MURDERERS
LYLE MENENDEZ

BY
EUGENE WEEMS

This book is based on real conversations and interactions with real notorious criminals in a variety of settings over a span of ten years. This book is intended as an educational tool only. The information given here is designed to help readers understand what actually transpires inside prison, and hopefully help those that are at-risk make informed decisions concerning their liberty and safety.

PRISON SECRETS

For information, go to: http://www.UniversalPublishingLLC.com

May be purchased for educational, business, or sales promotional use. For information, please write: Universal Publishing, LLC
                    Special Markets Department
                    P.O. Box 372
                    Port Orchard, WA 98366

Cover Design: Stephani Richardson
Editor: Terri Harper
        http://www.terristranscripts.net

ISBN: **978-0984045662**

Library of Congress Cataloguing-in-Publication Data: 2012933052

Universal Publishing, LLC

Printed in the United States of America

i

ACKNOWLEDGMENT

My deepest appreciation is extended to all those who had the audaciousness to help make this book a reality. I especially thank those who reached deep into their souls to find the integrity to deviate from the loyalty and define compulsory rules of their gangs in order to make a contribution to society for the edification of Prison Secrets. I realize that you have placed yourselves in grave danger by doing so. Trust and believe my Thank You is only a fraction of my appreciation, but I Thank You all once again.

CONTENTS

INTRODUCTION

"WARNING"

Please be advised to this warning of caution: As you venture beyond this INTRODUCTION you will actually be entering the gates into a world that you would find shocking, compelling and breathtaking that depicts the daily rituals beyond the imagination of the norm.

The language in this text is uncensored, vividly descriptive and may be found to be offensive to some readers. The author has chosen not to amend any of the contents, language or revealing events that he has experienced and been told about in order to provide the reader with a raw and truthful depiction and feeling of a prisoner's realization to a confined society that goes deeper than any imagination.

PRISON SECRETS
Eugene L. Weems

This book contains unexposed "Prison Secrets" the true facts as told by actual participants in leadership positions in the top nationally known prison and street gangs. Their identity has been withheld for security purposes in order to secure their safety and the safety of their family members from immediate or future retaliation by the gangs.

This book is the first of its kind that has the audaciousness to venture deep into the criminal mind and organizations of prison gangs, politics and activities behind the walls. Never has there been a book composed before this with such in-depth information, facts and extensive details of the sacred secrets of the prison gang operations, practices, racial outlooks, drug smuggling and distribution, alcohol manufacturing, weapons manufacturing, prison rape, and prison recipes. Everything you might want to know about prison and much more awaits you within these pages.

This literary composition exposes the true life behind the walls of the place society calls prison and prisoners call their reality. It was a vast research for the author to find prisoners in leadership positions who were not reluctant to abandon their loyalty to their gang and relinquish their sacred secrets in order for the development of this book that is directed toward introducing and informing society about the inhuman world that exists behind the prison walls.

This literary work has been a hostile and very dangerous study of the criminal minds behind the walls, but this book was certain to happen; it was imperative

2

that it be composed with attentiveness and carefully detailed information which would stand as a monumental and dominating source of edification and explanatory to the prison lifestyles and events.

PRISON SECRETS
Eugene L. Weems

MOTIVATING CIRCUMSTANCES

I, the author, decided that it was time for someone to step up to the plate and expose the secrets of the prison gangs and prison activities, so I took on the task to enter the arena myself in order to bring you (the reader) nothing but the truth. The actual ways how it goes down in these places known as prison, which I call the sinister beast, which are confined behind the walls are considered to be in the belly of the beast. This beast does partake of a pleasurable feast of gratification on a daily basis with human souls that become prey of the parasites that live in its belly. It digests the remains, keeping a regular bowel movement to make room for new potential prospects to be devoured and room new parasites to enter. The inmates are the parasites who keep this beast surviving with a constant flow of food. I could not trust anyone other than myself to tackle this project without being positive that you (the reader) would appreciate the authenticity of the beast's lifestyle.

The one thing that I found most difficult about composing this book was seeking the gang members from the different organizations to ask personal information about their gang functions and activities. Such inquiries could have gotten me stabbed and killed instantly by being so bold and inquisitive about things that don't concern me. It's not healthy at all to be prying into places that don't belong, but it was good on my behalf that I had what you would call a respectful convict relationship with the guys I approached with my request for information in order to bring this book about.

I pretty much felt someone was going to run back to their gang members and inform them what I was up to and order a hit on my life, but that never happened and it's a blessing that it hadn't. I was a damn fool to even approach them people like I had, but can assure you that I will never venture blindly down that road again like I had to establish this book. One time for me is too many, and a second time would be just plain ignorant, and ignorant is what I'm not. Deranged, yes, I would say so to a certain extent. Years spent living in the belly of the beast brings every one of its parasites to conform with its custom of behavior if you want to survive. What motivated me the most to get the information I needed for this book was concerns for the kids. I figured if teens had access to information like this book about the real lifestyle of prison and not the glamorized fictional version of it, just maybe it would divert them from being involved in gangs and criminal activity to avoid this inhuman lifestyle of violence, hatred, agony, disloyalty, misery, and the invidious torturous acts of the insane. I have seen so many that did come into the belly of the beast (prison) that would never see their freedom again and most of them became unsuspecting prey, condemned as a slave to cater to sexual desires or to be a flunky. There are so many vultures who lurk in the silent shadows of their own mind for such opportunity to present itself, and when it does, they strike with a convincing tongue and an aggressive demeanor to devour their prey's mind to refill it with wicked and deranged beliefs. Yes, it's sickening, but it's a reality of the prison lifestyle, just like many other things in the realm of its world.

I am sure this book would be of great assistance to law enforcement, federal, state, county and juvenile correctional facilities throughout the world, as well as legal practitioners, counselors, people who have family and friends inside the prisons, and those who are just curious about knowing the truth about the lifestyle.

Now that you have the facts, and raw and uncut truth about the prisons, you can no longer turn your head, ignore it or pretend it doesn't exist, say it can't happen to me or I would never go to prison. Well, hopefully you won't, but never say never because you never know what type of situation you might be placed in. You could be placed in a situation as I once was that landed me in prison. It was either do what I must to protect myself and family from being executed by gang members or just let them kill us all. Now what choice would you make? I did not have to ponder on such options for mine came naturally. Also, please don't adopt the impression that everyone in prison is bad or guilty of the crime they are in there for. There are a lot of innocent and good hearted people behind the walls and every story is different than the other. Some receive justice through the appeals courts and get out, while others may not be so fortunate and must continue up the ladder to the higher courts, which could take years before their cases are reviewed while an innocent person has to remain suffering from the distress, pain, restlessness and injured mentally from the lack of benevolent association, hoping that he receive justice from the higher courts.

I shall now escort you through the gates and into the realms behind prison walls from my personal experience and what I've witness as a prisoner. My eyes shall be your window to walk inside the prison so you could experience what I have and see firsthand what it's like, all from the comfort and safety of your home, office, or wherever you may be drifting your eyes attentively over these deep intense string of words. So please brace yourself as I now escort you through a prisoner's world.

***

WELCOME TO STATE PRISON the sign read that stood in the middle of a small patch of green grass that was neatly manicured at the entrance of the prison compound. The prison looked like a condemned hotel right out of a horror movie. Its dull white paint was peeling from its stony brick walls. The small narrow slits of what would be windows were bound with thick rusty bars that had been beaten by many years of the seasonal weather. The tall three layer fences with razor wire intertwined at the top surrounded every inch of the prison concrete foundation. There rested a warning sign on the middle fence that read, *Danger, this fence is electric.* Guard towers stood at every corner of the prison. Between the electric fence and the high power assault rifle that hung by a leather strap on the guards' shoulders, any attempted escapee wouldn't stand a chance of making it out alive. Each guard tower stood high above the prison. They looked like tree houses from a distance but without the limbs. They were shaped like huts with a round slope metal roof and a rusty bar railing that encircled its edges. Its Plexiglas windows were tinted dark black to keep wondering eyes from viewing inside. Two big search lights were embedded to the railing and a red eye on top of the tower windmilled at night. The towers were not secured within the prison fences, they stood several yards on the outskirts of each corner, and were high like miniature sky scrapers. They were unexposed and unthreatened by pedestrians or prisoners.

The gray goose prisoner transport bus came to a stop at the entrance gate of the prison. Two of the three escort officers exited the bus. One of them held a black pistol grip 12-gauge shoot gun in his hand while an assault rifle rested on his right shoulder. His partner carried a black utility belt on his shoulder and a black 45 automatic in his right hand. They ambled to the guard shack and vanished from sight, moments later reappearing empty handed. The utility belts they worn were no longer in their possession. Later down the line I learn that their weapons weren't allowed past prison gates once entering the compound.

The guards approached the bus and quickly began unlocking and opening up the bus storage compartments that held the prisoners' personal property, medical files and other unknown items. The guard shack officer immediately began inspecting the compartments. He toted a metal detector like device that had a circular shape mirror on the end of it that faced upward so he could view underneath the bus to check for contraband and explosive devices. He placed the gadget underneath the edge of the bus and swiftly made one complete inspection. After he finished, he signaled his approval with a wave of the hand. The other two officers quickly began securing the compartments, then re-entered the bus and waited for the first gate to open.

We entered and came to a halt. The gate began closing trapping the bus inside a small area. The three officers exited the bus and waved up at the distant tower, apparently a procedure to assure the tower officer that all three officers were safe. When they returned back inside, the second gate opened. We drove through and around to a building that sat high off the ground; seven concrete steps led to its dock. It seemed the building was used for loading and unloading, which it was because the back door of the main kitchen was approximately fifteen feet away. Eight officers stood outside awaiting our arrival. They all wore black jumpsuits, leather gloves and steel toe leather boots that were laced high on their shins. They had matching Teflon vests and head gear with Plexiglas face shields and thick black utility belts that hosted many different gadgets. They stood in solidarity holding a side handle PR-24 baton in their right hand and a canister of OC pepper spray in the other, except for one a sergeant who cradled a pistol grip 12-gauge shotgun that shoots rubber bullets.

One of the escort officers exited the bus and greeted the other officers with a nod, while the other two began unlocking the two cage doors that had separated us from the cockpit. The stench of stale warm urine from the bus urinal quickly engulfed the fresh air that had been blowing from the bus air condition before the sudden stop to depart. The hard plastic two man seat had deprived me of the feelings in my legs and my buttocks was throbbing with a terrible feeling of soreness. The shackles on my ankles and wrists were cutting into my Skin, causing the areas to become tender and to swell. The belly chain that was wrapped around my waist, bolted with a small padlock, rested snug up against my upper rib cage, making it difficult to breath. I sat on the bus motionless, shackled to another inmate who was anticipating the departure from the bus and shackles. The rubber texture shoes, which was more like a slip-on sandal plus shower shoe in one, rested uncomfortable on my numb feet. The smell of its rubbery odor was strong.

The bus was full with inmates; most of them were first timers like me who didn't know what to expect once behind prison walls. Not a word was spoken among the prisoners. The silence was loud and the racing heartbeats sounded like African drums beating in a rhythmic tune. One of the officers made his way to the back of the bus and broke the silence. "When I call out your last name, tell me your first," he demanded with an authoritative voice. He called out each name one at a time, and when he received a reply he would glance at the picture that was attached to what looked like an index card that he held in his hand. After he finished, we were ordered off the bus and instructed to line up single file. I exited the bus as quickly as I could. My legs were still asleep and I dragged my numb feet. My knees felt rubbery and felt like they would collapse at any moment. I carefully stepped off the bus, still shackled to another inmate who was now assisting me along the way.

"What the hell are you looking at, boy?" The deep voice echoed. I took a quick glance to see who the question was being directed to. I noticed an officer had stepped out of formation from his peers. He stormed toward his mark and got two inches from his face. "Boy, why were you staring at me? Do you have a problem with me, and do I look like someone you know?" He shouted harshly. The young frail man didn't answer; he stood shivering and in shock. He faced straight forward at the chest and neck of the six feet, three inch, two hundred fifty plus pound guard in the black jumpsuit. There wasn't one officer out of the eight who was under six feet tall and two hundred twenty-five pounds. It was obvious they were in good physical condition. This was our first lesson in proper behavior.

We were directed to go inside the building where there seemed to be an army of the black suited officers waiting inside for our arrival. They all stood in a single file line ready to attack on the spur of the moment. Two of them stepped out from the formation and began unchaining us one at a time. "Once unchained, step to the back wall and face it," One of them said. "You first two guys," he pointed toward the inmates he just un-cuffed. "Grab the wall and lift your right foot up." He then began removing the ankle shackles. Grab the wall? Did he mean place our hands on the wall? I dared not ask him for clarification. They both worked swiftly in sequence removing the enslavement devices, but not quickly enough to my preference. "You first two guys turn around and strip down." The first two inmates complied quickly, liberating the royal blue paper thin nylon fabric jumpsuits from their bodies. They stood nude awaiting further instructions. "Now open your mouth wide and run your forefinger around the rim of your mouth. Now run your hands through your hair three times. Okay, let me see your hands. Lift your arms high in the air. Now lift up your nut sacks. Turn around and let me see the bottom of your feet, starting with the right foot." He paused to catch a breath, never once dropping his attentive gaze. "Now bend over and spread your butt cheeks, squat and cough three times."

We were all subjected to the same body search. We stood nude with our hands behind our backs until the completion of the body searches. We faced the officers as if we were having a standoff. An officer pushed in a laundry cart and issued each of us a bed roll and orange jumpsuit. The bed roll consisted of one dark gray wool blanket, two dingy white sheets, and one white bath towel. The orange two piece jumpsuit had CDC (California Department of Corrections) with *prisoner* written on the back of the shirt and down the leg of the pants. The jumpsuit top was sleeveless and the pants had an elastic waistband and a back pocket. The uniform was made of 65% polyester and 35% cotton; it was constructed for longevity, I assured myself. It was accompanied by a pair of white socks, boxer shorts and a T-shirt. We were then issued a pair of slip-on jack flaps, which was shoes with a one-quarter inch plastic rubberized sole and a thin black textile fabric that covered the shoe. We dressed in our new prison attire.

One at a time we were directed to a small office were a prison nurse sat with an open file and a pen asking medical and mental health questions that she read from a list and made notes on. After her evaluation she requested my arm to give a tuberculosis shot. I was nervous allowing the nurse to stick a needle into my arm to administer the cloudy substance that was now being injected underneath my skin. I watched with uncertainty as the small area on my arm rose from the liquid. The nurse removed the needle from my skin while gently pressing a cotton swab over the area. Then she taped it onto my skin to hold it in place. "I will come and check your arm in three days to make sure you haven't been exposed to tuberculosis," she said. The thought of being contaminated didn't sit right with me. I tensed up at the thought.

After everyone went through the same medical ritual we were taken into another area to be photographed. One at a time we stood up with our backs against the wall holding a white eight by eleven card stock sideways directly underneath our chin. The card stock had featured my full name and prisoner number that had been computer generated. An officer stood only a few feet away aiming a funny shaped camera. A red beam of light protruded from it found a target somewhere between the bridge of my nose and my lips. I hadn't realized that I had stopped breathing until the flash on the camera slightly blurred my vision and then I inhaled and strongly exhaled, finding my normal breathing cycle.

After we were issued our identification card, we were escorted to a cage that resembled a pigeon coop. The square box shaped compartment was enclosed with a steel screen that had been painted blue on the outside. The inside revealed its original raw rust. There were wooden benches lined around the sides with two rows of benches that sat in the middle floor, facing the cage door. In each corner of the cage you could see the big bolts that had been drilled into the concrete to keep the steel cage in place. A huge metal fan rested high embedded against a brick wall with its rotating blades spinning at a high speed, sending a cool breeze directly into the cage where I rested my back up against its surface. I probed the facial expressions of the restless, which walked around anticipating what would be

15

demanded of them next. I was tired, exhausted mentally, and physically drained by the long hours spent traveling on the bus. My eyes felt heavy, but I forced myself to remain wide awake and observant of my surroundings.

An officer appeared with an inmate worker in tow carrying a big clear plastic garbage bag full of brown paper sack lunches. He unlocked the grill gate and issued them out. I quickly dug into the lunch and it seemed that everyone else had followed my lead or I was following theirs. Either way, we all was now assaulting the sack to reach what it concealed inside its paper protection. I tilted my sack upside down, dumping the contents onto the wood bench. I didn't have the patience for the suspense to remove the items one at a time from the bag. I was famished and ready to devour whatever food items the sack contained. A small apple rushed out leading the pack, introducing itself as the only nutritious substance in the bag. A pack of wheat bread with four individual slices followed, then a pack of meat, a pack of two sugar cookies the size of a silver dollar, and two mustard condiments laid in a pile next to me. I wasted no time undressing the items. I ate greedily with attentive eyes monitoring the inmates. Paranoia had settled in that was now directing my behavior. Moments later, the same officer appeared and announced, "Gentlemen, before you step out, make sure you haven't left any trash behind you. As you go out the door I want you to make a left and line up against the wall single file. There is a waste basket by the wall you can dump your trash in," I remembered him saying and added, "No talking out in the halls gentlemen!" The cage door opened and we rushed through. I waited until everyone was out before exiting.

There were four separate cages in the hallway lined up against the wall. Each one was singled off approximately four feet from each other. It contained one long wooden bench within its boundary and only enough room to sit. There were two single man cages that were screened with Plexiglas and which were designed for only standing. One at a time we were called into an office to undergo questioning by the classification sergeant. "What gang you run with? Do you have any tattoos? Do you have any problems with being in general population?" I recalled him asking. Once he was through with his questioning he handed me a piece of paper with a unit and cell number on it. I ambled out the office and an officer directed me to my destination. I was greeted at the unit door by two officers, one who requested to see my prison ID and who manually logged our information on a sheet of paper that was being held in place by the spring clip of a brown clip board. The unit was deafening, the inmates was shouting across the tier socializing, acting a damn fool, talking over each other. Some inmates were singing while others used their cell door as a drum. Trash and dirty laundry littered the bottom tier. The officer pointed up toward my assigned cell and my eyes followed his finger. The other officer returned my identification card, and I made my way up the flights of stairs to the third floor.

The door of my assigned cell was half the size of a regular house door, which reminded me of a kid's playhouse door but only taller. There was a square bar window that was missing the bottom Plexiglas. One of the officers came to key the door. I had to turn sideways to step inside. The stench of backed up sewage, rust, sweat mingling in a humid room twisted my stomach and face into a knot. I flared my nose in pure disgust of the cell. A porcelain bowl and toilet, which was stained permanently by filth impurities that had been constantly neglected of a sanitary cleaning. The brick walls were decorated in graffiti, names of gangs and nicknames of the members who occupied the room before me. Ants paraded up the back wall and out the missing back window. Cockroaches remained out in the open and seemed unintimidated by my presence. Quiet as it was, I was intimidated and had every reason to be. They didn't act or look like any ordinary cockroaches that I had seen. If I didn't know any better, I would have sworn they were little body builders with attitudes. I cast a momentary gaze over the floor to take inventory of the brown vermin insect gang. I spotted a few more that had gone unnoticed during my first sweep of the cell. There were others posted in crevices and corners of the room. I followed my better judgment and just stepped around the ones who seemed to have something to prove. It was only obvious that the cell was constructed to house only one person, but all the different lives that it contained only made things that much more complex. Two humans and several dozen insects battling for territory just weren't happening. I later found out we had burglars, when I saw a rat come up under the door that looked up at me as if I was the one invading his house. After I thought about it, I was.

A slab of concrete rose several feet from the floor, six feet in length with a thin mattress on top that was constructed to be a bunk that my cellie occupied. On the opposite wall there was a slab of metal the same length as the concrete bunk. It was folded up against the wall secured at the middle by a thick chain. Some inventive person had figured out a way to add another bunk into a cell that was already crowded for standing, let alone housing two people. I released the contraption of its security device, guiding the heavy metal to the floor. I noticed the white cotton pinstriped twin mattress that it had been concealing. I carefully inspected the mattress for foulness before dressing it with clean linen.

My cellie was a first timer like myself so he didn't say much or ask personal questions. My conversation was condensed as well. The forty-five day stay in the reception center was just the introduction to the hellish life of prison. Every day was monotonous, confined to the cell, no television, magazines, board games, music, nothing for entertainment. Just me, my cellie and the unwanted insects who became my enemies the first night of my stay after sending me and my cellie seeking medical attention after they wined and dined on our bodies. A hydrocortisone cream and calamine lotion became our bodies' defense mechanism at night as we waged battle against the insects during the day. I prayed silently that the prison I would be endorsed to wasn't like this reception center.

My time was expired and I had been endorsed to a maximum security prison that catered to my sentence structure. *Damn*, I thought. *I'm heading to the top of the ladder without climbing up the steps. A place were all the killers and toughest of the tough criminal reside.* I tried not to think about it, but my mind was controlling itself and that was the only topic it gave any attention.

I was transferred to another prison. The bus ride was painful and three times longer than the first. I had to undergo the same type of initial treatment I had before with the enslavement devices, nurse and being processed into a new institution, but the only difference this time, I had to submit to more than one photograph. The prison required a photo that could be downloaded into a computer, so with their handheld digital camera they effortlessly zoomed in on my facial features and robbed me of an expression that I would never be able to get back, and if I could, I was sure that I didn't want it. Instead of orange two-piece jumpsuit, I was issued a white one-piece jumpsuit and a bedroll that contained the same type of wool blanket, white towel, pair of boxer shorts, socks, t-shirt, two blue sheets and a clear sack with a plastic cup and spoon, a 6 oz. tube of toothpaste, a two-inch tooth brush, a small comb, and a hotel size bar of soap. After I was cleared from R&R (Receiving and Releasing), I was escorted to an assigned yard and housing unit. I was placed in a cell by myself. A sign was placed on the outside of the door that indicated that

I was on orientation and first had to go in front of a classification committee before being allowed out of the cell to program with the general population.

One of the first things I noticed when I entered the cell was that it was a lot bigger than the one I had recently been in. No broken window and a much better setup. I glanced around the floor for any sight of insects. I sighed in relief when there wasn't any. The floor was a smooth concrete surface that seemed to have been waxed and buffed. It gave off a mirror reflection of the cell's interior. The door was a normal size that had a rectangle shaped window and a tray slot that could only be keyed open from the outside. The door was controlled by the unit tower officer and had to be slid open. The cell had bunk beds bolted against the wall right over each other, and a metal desk with a stool that extended out from underneath the desk, on a metal bar that was also bolted against the wall. There were two metal shelves on the opposite wall from the bunks, and a one-piece stainless steel sink and toilet. I listened to the drone of the air conditioner that was blowing furiously from a vent. I heard faintly the sounds of a television program in the next cell. The cell was clean and seemed to have been recently painted sandy gray. Each bunk had a thin plastic green mattress on its surface.

Inmates approached my cell and asked what seemed like a thousand and one personal questions, of which I only answered about five. A few offered canteen and hygiene items and the use of books and magazines, but I respectfully rebuffed the gesture. Every inmate that came to my cell door presented a look of urgency and a facial expression that was being weighted down by earth's gravity. I saw in their eyes the longing of a smile that had met its demise somewhere in the past of their incarceration and I wondered if my own appearance would someday only offer an unsympathetic look and a demeanor too serious for relaxation, a reality I knew I had to avoid falling prey to.

In eight days I was in front of a classification committee, who shuffled through files that lay on the desk. They reviewed a report that detailed my history, and recommended I take employment as a program clerk or teacher aid. The sound of employment sounded excellent and beneficial in more ways than financial gain, until I inquired into the starting salary that would be offered. When I heard the words *cents per day*, I had no reason to consider the number that was said before those words. My mind took on a blank. Working for pennies was out of the question and I expressed it with an unseen exclamation point after my words. What the hell did I look like, working for pennies after I had paid my way through college to obtain a degree in business, just to work in some body prison. *These people was out of their damn mind,* I thought.

"Those who don't take up a job or attend school don't receive the full benefit of the recreation program," the program captain said, probing my face for any sign that I would change my mind. Somehow I managed to keep a straight face that offered him no indication to the disrespect I was now feeling. The counselor mentioned something about placing me on a support list before pushing several pieces of paper toward me gently. I picked them up and swiftly glanced over them. One was just a notice that the interview took place and the other was a laundry slip to receive my state issue.

I respectfully departed and made my way out of the building to the laundry. I was given the standard issue: three white t-shirts, three boxer shorts, six pair of socks, a belt, three light blue long sleeve button-up shirts, two sheets, one towel, two laundry bags - one for whites, the other for blues, a jacket, and a pair of black and white generic all-stars sneakers.

That night, I received a cellie who had come from another prison. He was a veteran to the prison lifestyle and was incarcerated for many years. When he approached my cell door, he didn't wait to be asked questions. He offered answers sharply and precisely to normally asked questions of new roommates and waited for my approval to be allowed into my cell. It wasn't that he was intimidated by me. The reason he didn't just barge in the room without my approval is because I might not have wanted to accept a roommate, and when an inmate overlooks those whishes, then a knife or a killing could be his punishment for his disrespect. Respect inside the prison is mandatory if you were to continue to breathe. I allowed him to move in.

The veteran turned out to be a solid cat, who laced my shoes on how to make weapons out of just about anything; and he taught me the secrets of staying alive and not becoming someone's victim. *Never be too quick* *to speak; learn to listen. Don't trust no one but yourself. Regardless of how cool you and the person are, no one is to be trusted. Never expose personal information; keep a mask on so people can't figure you out. Remove all addresses from your personal letters and don't share your personal photos with anyone. Also don't have anyone make phone calls for you. Never accept nothing from no one for free, and don't borrow or loan anyone anything. And number one rule of all, mind your own business. I don't give a damn if you see oil shooting out of the ground. Mind your own business. You see it but you don't see it, and if someone ever threatens your life, don't take it lightly, react on it immediately regardless, he* said coldly. He didn't give me any explanation behind his advice and I didn't ask for any either. Common sense provided some of the answers, but observing others who done all the things I was warned not to do answered the rest of my unasked questions.*

It had become clear to me that the life behind the walls was a cruel, merciless and a brutal place. Additionally, it had unfolded right before my eyes the myriad of demons that was trapped in human bodies. My environment began to have an invidious effect on my way of thinking and cheerful personality. I noticed my smile had lost its elevation without warning.

I had been on the main line for two weeks and had already seen a lifetime of events and violent activities: homosexuals room hopping, inmates shooting dope sharing the same needle, inmates sharpening up knifes that looked more like a sword than a knife, inmates making white lightning, a crew running into a cell and savagely beating an inmate with batteries in a sock while some stomped and kicked him. I've seen hot water mixed with baby oil dashed in another inmate's face that immediately peeled his skin back. Each day presented another violent act to add to my collection of memories.

The captain hadn't lied about my program would be limited. I wasn't receiving much outside yard time. I was released out to the yard every other day for two and a half hours, and that depended if the institution count was cleared. The yard had no weights, only monkey bars for the inmate monkeys who wanted to swing on it, pull and lower themselves on, and from the look of it, they were content. The basketball court remained packed with Africans playing prison ball. Everything goes except for groping below the waist. The handball courts stayed occupied with Woods on one side and Northerners on the other. Southerners made their mark on the soccer field. The others played volleyball with any race who wanted to play, which is usually the Woods. The Muslims stood posted in a designated area they marked as their territory, viewing the activity on the yard. Groups of no less than three circled the small dirt track. It was mandatory by all races and gangs that no one should be walking or working out alone. The Crips was bunched up around a concrete bench table they claimed and identified it as the gambling shack and nothing but smoking weed and gambling went on over there. A domino game was being played at one end, chess game in the middle and a pinochle game at the other end. A crowd crouched in a circle shooting dice. I figured since

25

everyone else was claiming things that really didn't belong to them, I would do the same, so I claimed the punching bag that seems to have been neglected before I befriended it.

"Yard down! Yard down!" The tower officer yelled over the yard intercom following a heart shocking explosion. "Everyone get down, now!" I didn't know what to do; the eruption of the gun had startled my common sense. For some reason my mind was digressing back to the signs that were posted throughout the prison that said there would be no warning shots! Another burst of explosion roared and rumbled like thunder. "Everyone get down! Yard is down!" The warning gun officer snapped harshly again. I quickly came to my senses and dove to the damp grass, then immediately examined my surrounding. The yard was in an uproar. A full riot was in progress, and I mean a full riot. The Africans, Caucasian and Mexicans were violently striking each other in the facial and upper torso area. Those that lost their footing were rat packed and kicked violently. The inmates stabbed each other with crudely designed weapons. The second response officers were called in. They were in full battle gear when they rushed into the heat of things utilizing their side handle baton and MK-9 pepper spray trying to diffuse the action. Inmates began stabbing them. Then a rapid fire of explosions erupted all around the yard as canisters of tear gas burst among the crowds. Unknown objects whistled pass my head into the ground, kicking up the earth's soil before my very eyes. Inmates met the barrel of a direct blast from a block gun. Every unit tower officers was hanging out the window rapidly firing their block gun and high power rifles.

I covered my head using my hands and forearms as a shield to protect it from the projectiles that zipped through the atmosphere like falling stars. Panic suggested that I get up and make a break back to the unit. Then somewhere hidden in the darkness of my mind, ignorance advised me to just jump up and get involved in the thick of things, participate, use that knife you have on you, stab someone, anyone, a cop if you can; that would really get you the utmost respect of the inmates. I grimaced at the thought. *Fuck respect. I'm not about to do no stupid shit like that, you stupid mothafucka.* I blurted out angrily at my thoughts as if we weren't one and the same. *Just be cool and stay put and toss that knife you have on you,* my emotions warned me. That was a more logical suggestion. Then I tossed the knife away from me. The officers had the yard under control and when the smoke cleared there were many seriously hurt and no one could receive any medical attention until the yard was secured and everyone was placed in flex cuffs and searched. Death was sure to claim some lives.

The MTA responding staff set up folding tables in front of the program offices and the officers escorted inmates a few at a time for medical evaluations. This process took hours. A group of other officers taped off the crime scene where knifes were found and inmates lay deceased or seriously injured while one officer walked around with a video camera filming every inmate. Once the yard was cleared of all involved inmates, responding staff escorted the suspected and injured inmates, lined them up against the wall of the program building and escorted them one after the other to the facility health services for further medical evaluation and decontamination from the effects of OC exposure. After being attended to by the medical staff, all the suspected involved inmates were escorted and temporarily re-housed in their assigned cells without further incident. I still felt the butterflies in the pit of my gut when I made it back to my cell. I paced the cell floor for several hours. Chow never came and the night was escaping into a different day.

Two officers came to my door and told me to turn around and cuff up. I asked why. "You were seen by staff tossing a weapon on the yard during the incident," one of them said. *Damn! Man!* That's all I could utter under my breath to myself. *I thought I was in the clear when I made that move. I should have just used the mothafucka,* I told myself out of anger and frustration.

I was taken to the hole, strip searched and placed in a cell in my underclothes and shower shoes. That was the only clothing allowed. Canteen was once every month and there was a limit on how much you could spend and certain items you could purchase. All food items were opened in front of me and repackaged in clear Ziploc bags. Toothpaste was squeezed out from its tube into a small bag; deodorant was removed from its container and bagged. I was not allowed to purchase lotion, baby oil or hair products. There was no human contact or coming out your cell for tier time. One fifteen minute shower every 72 hours and I was handcuffed and escorted to and from the shower. Nothing to look at but the walls around me or the wall that's right outside my door. There was no back window to look through to the outside, no way for the sun rays to shine in on you, nothing but the brick walls. There was a small window constructed into the ceiling that the officers could look down inside the cell. The room temperature stayed at an unpleasant cold sensation and its chilliness mocked my shivers. My only entertainment was the voice of other inmates on the tier and my daydreams which I indulged in for days at a time.

My mind started to play tricks on me. My eyes purposely gazed at the brick wall that held my body imprisoned within its protective boundaries. My ears absorbed the steady fluent flow of sentences that been composed with a combination of carefully selected words, depicting a story about a Las Vegas pimp named Break a Hoe, that my neighbor had written, basically on the lines of his own life before his incarceration. As my conscious mind concentrated on the sequence of the words, I began to feel a hypnotic effect beginning its course. Slowly my mind's eye took on a tunnel vision with swirls of fog closing in from all sides. I could still hear my neighbor's spoken words, but only vaguely due to the state that my conscious level was adopting that denied me access to the clarity of their meaning. As my subconscious being took control, my mind's eye flashed back to a spiritual plain the revilement of my struggles of the fight from the demons within that was viewed with vivid clarity. The war to free my soul from sin was

29

rehashed before my very eyes. It's like I was a male version of Dorothy, only this was not OZ, and I had never before experienced such dilemma as this until now.

The first thing that hit me was like a vortex, sucking away all the oxygen out of my lungs and surroundings. I was in a cold sweat and my heart beat violently against my deflated chest in a plea for help from being suffocated by the poignant highly toxic stench of sulfur, on a scale far surpassed by a million decayed corpses. The intense burning of my lungs with every inhale I attempted caused me to wretch uncontrollably. I tried crying to God, and several times I heard myself calling out for momma over Him. In the distant background of this putrid odor was an underlying scent that my sinuses at first weren't able to decipher. Then like a déjà vu, my internal alarm warned me that the smell was sizzling flesh being mixed with rotten and decayed corpses of the damned. The combination was enough to drive any mortal being to the point of hysteria and arouse the feeling of vomiting, but being that I was in between the unconscious world and a spirit form, nothing solid came forth from my mouth. It was hard to breathe due to the gaseous texture and lack of oxygen brought about by hell fire's magmas that were already feeding and devouring all it came into contact with and releasing toxins that should have claimed my life but miraculously failed to do so. I tried calling anyone on the tier, but no one responded. I even used racial slurs in the most disrespectful way just to get a response, but no one said anything. I screamed to see if I could hear myself, but my ears were filled with cries of the damned that intermingled with the legions of demons. The lost souls that were once confined, as I screeched, their miseries and their tormented wailings reached out to my soul which was already overwhelmed by all the anguish my spirit was feeling. I felt that I was being drowned in a tidal wave of vibes that were so apparently clear to my ears that touched my soul deeply within, with heart wrenching sorrow and an unexplainable fear. I attempted to block it out, but even if I was deaf it would no more decrease in volume. The horrific pleas from the condemned for relief from the torment inflicted upon them due to the hardened hearts they possessed as they dwelled on the face of the earth, living it up with sin's pleasure while brushing off the Lord's warnings of what consequences they would receive for not repenting.

I wondered what it all had to do with me. Then Satan's whispers penetrated my thoughts, filling my subconscious being with his lies and deceptions of what wickedness has doomed my soul to. He replenished my sight with lust of mankind's treasures in an effort to break the gossamer threads of hope I possessed of regaining my freedom and holding onto my morals and sanity. Satan quickly tried to place a veil over my eyes to blind me of the joys, the love that God has destined our hearts to experience. The ever-present myriads of demons relaying Satan's lies about there being no escape, no turning back from the clutches of hell, and I must conform and be the best killer, predator, the top dog of my race, lead the masses and gain the power to make history. Don't follow no rules but the ones you set. I cried out for momma as if I was once again that infant she raised into a man. Devilish, sinister laughter came to me in rippling waves throughout the atmosphere, attacking my senses. I was now feeling more than hearing. I heard so many voices at once, and not being able to separate them individually, just all traveling in waves, sending quivers through the core of my bones and drowning me with a feeling of suffocation. I deeply and violently gasped for breath, only to choke on the poisonous gasses created from the beds of brimstone and fire while that wicked laugh expressed its joy at seeing my suffering. The laughter came to my ears so vividly with crystalline clarity that brought goose bumps to my spiritual flesh. And the higher I climbed, the more intensified the atmosphere throbbed with Satan's hatred that was now hitting me in shock waves as phantoms flew throughout my body.

A steady drone sounded that immediately brought the taunting faces to a halt, a sound of authority that I didn't understand at the time until I felt Satan's telekinetic powers being aimed at my mind, replaying the evil that I have done in my past. The innocent people who became my victims during my hustling and all my deeds that constitute surviving at any means necessary. The backsliding and rejection I've had for the Lord was now in the front of my thoughts. All those visions flashed through my mind, yet I still struggled toward the exit, fighting off the evil that was trying to hinder my efforts to live. I struggled for every inch, feeling my body quickly dwindling in strength as Satan lashed out at me with a massive forked tongue of flames that took hold to my ankle and like a whip, wrapped itself around me with a firm grip, making it impossible to gain any more ground. I kicked at this grip just to lose my footing, and on my way falling back down into his fire pit I said a serious prayer asking God for a second chance.

I suddenly realized my prayer was heard. I had snapped back into reality, noticing my body was drenched in perspiration, where my spirit had been on a journey to its demise, and that very moment I dropped to my knees and prayed in the realms of reality. My neighbor's voice could be heard clearly once again as he continued to entertain the tier with his street story. I looked down at my makeshift calendar I made, totaling up the days I have been locked away in a dungeon for three months and counting.

I tremored as if I had Parkinson's, while taking a bird bath out of the sink. After I finished, I went to lie down on the bunk but was too afraid to close my eyes or concentrate on any area of the room for long, especially after what had just occurred. I took inventory of my personal thoughts as to how I was going to free myself from this world of imprisonment, but came up with no answers.

The next day I went in front of a classification committee. I was found not guilty of tossing a weapon and was sent back to the main line. It's amazing how a person can appreciate all the things he takes for granted until they are taken away from him. I smiled up at the sun and shaded my eyes with my hand; its warm rays smothered the chills, caressing my skin. I inhaled the fresh air slowly, holding it captured in my lungs longer than average, and after my lungs became intimate with it, I released it back into the atmosphere. I even smiled down at the cricket that was chirping where I stood appreciating the outdoors. I took my time going to my new assigned housing unit.

Nothing had changed but a few new faces and a few absent ones. I was back in the swing of things. I learned new tricks of the prison trade. Like for instance, how to iron your clothes with a soap dish and crease them with a comb, how to fold them and place them under your mattress to give it a pressed look. Inmates used their toilet or a five pound paint bucket to wash their personal clothes. I watched an old timer beat down four dudes after rubbing Ben Gay cream all over his hands first and went for their facial area, a trick I came to learn to be useful when you knew that the fight will be uneven. Once the Ben Gay gets into the eyes of your opponent, the fight is basically over. You can't hit what you can't see.

I was slowly becoming part of my environment. I indulged in the selling of drugs. The money was needed to purchase legal books, pay for legal assistance, typing, postage and personal necessities. I start forming a crew who I trained in the art of kick boxing, being that I was a professional fighter who competed for prize money in the underground tough man competitions before my incarceration. Most of my crew members were eighteen to twenty seven years old who weren't involved with any prison gangs. We functioned as a team and were each other's comforter. Our days consisted of working out, intellectual meetings of the minds and constant educational studies. Hustling was top priority for we all had a common goal, our freedom, and the finances had to be made. We had no family support, so we became each other's family. We would sell shots of coffee, which is a tablespoon full, for a stamp, finger of tobacco for one dollar or three stamps. A finger of tobacco is tobacco that is placed in a plastic glove and each finger of that glove is removed and tied. The one dollar is not actual paper money. It is an item of food or hygiene that's worth a dollar or more of a trade. We read and wrote letters for inmates who didn't know how to read or write.

Although I stayed busy, prison lifestyle was taking a dramatic toll on my entity, and viewing all the things that went on inside and seeing the young kids and adults who couldn't protect themselves physically from the abuse of the predators that roamed the prison compound, I became disgusted, frustrated, feeble in my spirit and hopes. Mainly I endured enough of this hatred world of prison. The thought of why I was incarcerated settled into my mind and I decided to create "Prison Secrets" to expose the game and to help the kids and teens in society correct their criminal behaviors by giving them a look into the real life of prison and all that it has to offer anyone who's sentence to prison. It is not a boot camp or like a jail; it is actually hell.

PRISON SECRETS
Eugene L. Weems

CHAPTER 1

DRUG SMUGGLING AND DISTRIBUTION

Drugs inside the prison are a lucrative commodity and are always in a high demand. The inmates who are in the smuggling, distribution and sales will go through any drastic measures to get the narcotics into the prisons regardless of the circumstances they must face. Selling drugs inside of the prison is a lot of inmates' livelihood, and their means to obtain life necessities and the luxuries of what prison has to offer to them. It's all about the money and having a supply of drugs to meet the demands.

In this chapter you will learn all the secrets on how drugs are smuggled into the prisons. You will learn their selling prices and the methods of payment, the types of drugs being brought into the prisons and all the places that the drugs are hidden, then how they are distributed. Every aspect of smuggling and distribution of drugs inside the prisons will be covered from A to Z within this chapter. There will be no stone left unturned.

DRUG ENTERPRISE

Every prison gang faction deals in the smuggling and selling of drugs either to support their gang or just to indulge themselves with the substance of choice. On every yard there is always one big dope dealer who supplies the prison hustlers who are dedicated money seekers and does not use drugs himself other than marijuana, if that. These hustlers are normally members of gangs who are dedicated to keeping a constant flow of drugs coming into the prison, and nine out of ten, the head dope man will be an African American because many of the Africans do not use the hard drugs that are at a demand inside of the prisons. Additionally, they do not discriminate to who they sell to, unlike the southern Mexicans who will not sell to the Africans or the northern Mexicans and will not buy from them. If a southern Mexican is a drug user and his supply of drugs runs out, some will sneak and buy drugs from other races without it being known to their race.

The prison hustlers are the yard's small time dope men who make direct sales to the inmate population. Although they may be small time compared to the yard's big dope man who normally supplies them with the drugs, the hustler's profits are much larger than that of the big dope man's, but their risks are much higher as well. The reason for that is because the big dope man only sells his drugs in bulk quantity to his hustlers and personal acquaintances to avoid the risk of being busted. His goal is to make a quick profit without the wait and the problems. He knows the hustler's money is good because they pay up front or in advance, which limits his risk and allows him to get off the product immediately and make his money behind the scene. The hustlers are the ones who take the risk of being exposed by inmates, busted with drugs, inmates locking up in PC (Protective Custody) because they can't pay their debts.

DISTRIBUTION

The hustlers are the ones who distribute the drugs to the inmates. They don't sell the drugs in bulk, only in small amounts (papers & caps). The papers range in price depending on the size of the paper and the type of product that is being sold. A paper is a small quantity of a drug wrapped or sealed in plastic or placed in a paper made bindle which the inside surface is lined with clear tape. A cap is a Chap Stick cap amount of a substance that is placed in a paper bindle or sealed in clear plastic, usually marijuana.

TYPES OF DRUGS AND PRICES

The most popular drugs in prison are heroin, methamphetamine, cocaine, crack cocaine and marijuana. The prison population has its own slang to identify each drug. The following are examples of commonly used prison terminology that refers to each drug.

Cocaine: baby powder, powder, white, white girl, snow.

Crack Cocaine: candy, marble, pebble, rock, stone.

Heroin: black, black girl, burger, smack, tar.

Marijuana: bud, Christmas tree, clover, greenery, mint leaf, money green, smoke, tree.

Methamphetamine: crank, crystal, glass, go fast, hype, speed, white sinister.

STREET PRICES

The following prices are references for an ounce (28 grams). These are street prices in society and some places the prices may be cheaper or a little higher than the below quoted prices. This information is important to give you (the reader) a keen understanding on how profitable drugs are inside the prisons.

Products	Half Ounce
Cocaine	$450-500
Crack Cocaine	$450-500
Heroin	$600-900
Marijuana	$35-40
Methamphetamine	$450-600

PRISON PRICES

The prison's top dope man only sells ounces of marijuana. He will only sell ounces, halves and quarters of cocaine, crack cocaine and methamphetamine, and only grams of heroin to the yard hustlers (the distributors) and his own personal customers.

Products	Ounce	½ oz.	¼ oz.	Gram
Cocaine	$2000	$1000	$500	NA
Crack Cocaine	$2000	$1000	$500	NA
Heroin	NA	NA	NA	$150-200
Marijuana	$150-200	NA	NA	NA
Methamphetamine	$2000	$1000	$500	NA

The prices charged by the hustler (distributor) who sells to the prison population are a lot different. These quoted prices are the same throughout the prisons.

Cocaine costs $500 per quarter ounce and is sold in papers for $50 each. A quarter ounce makes 42 papers. Total value, $2,100 per quarter ounce, or $1,600 profit potential.

Crack Cocaine costs $500 per quarter ounce and is sold by the stone. Each stone sells for $100. A quarter ounce (7 grams) cuts into 15 stones. Total value, $1,500 per quarter, or $1,000 profit potential.

Heroin costs $150-200 per gram and is sold in papers. Each paper is the size of a wooden match stick and costs $50. A gram of heroin makes sixteen papers. Total value, $800, or $650 profit potential. Some hustlers will sell quarter grams for $100, which is still $250 profit potential for a gram purchased for $150.

Marijuana costs $150-200 per ounce and is sold by the cap. Each Chap Stick cap sells for $10. One ounce of marijuana makes a minimum of 60 caps. Total value, $600 per ounce, or $400 profit potential.

Methamphetamine, costs $500 per quarter ounce and is sold in papers for $50 each. A quarter ounce makes 42 papers. Total value, $2,100 per quarter ounce, or $1,600 profit potential.

METHODS OF PURCHASING DRUGS

The drugs are given to the inmates on consignment and an agreement to the method and the time period of paying. If the inmate doesn't pay the money by the agreed deadline, the amount owed is doubled and the inmate is given another time period to get the money to its destination. If he fails, then several things will happen. He would be demanded to give up everything in his cell that's worth the amount he owes or he would become a victim of violence, or both.

The inmate drug dealer usually has an outside correspondent that collects and holds his money. He provides the inmate buyer with a name and address where he wants the money to go. Usually this address is a P.O. Box. The buyer would have his outside correspondent Western Union the money or send a money order directly to the address. If the inmate buyer chooses not to use an outside correspondent or can't rely on his correspondence to send the money or meet the designated timeframe, he would fill out a trust withdraw slip with the prison to have the money that is owed withdrawn from his prison account. The prison would send out a prison check to the party the inmate requested it to be sent to.

Then you have the prison canteen, which is a fast way to pay and collect a debt. The drug dealer makes out a list of items he prefers from the store and gives it to the buyer, who purchases those items from the prison canteen and gives them to the dealer. A lot of times a drug dealer would expect new postage stamps and items from a quarterly package, shoes, clothes etc. They even would accept whatever that is of value. It's all about negotiating.

Inmates who get visits would have their visitors bring them cash money and they would either pay the dealer if he's out in the visiting room or smuggle the money back inside the prison and pay him then.

SMUGGLING

The visiting room is the main vehicle how drugs enter the prisons. The inmate who carry the drugs from the visiting room are called *Mules*. The mules prepare in advance before going out into the visiting room by lubricating his anus with some type of lubrication, petroleum jelly, hair dressing, or whatever that's available at the time. There are always mules out in the visiting room that are willing to assist anyone who needs his service. The mules are identified by wearing his prison jacket, a signal known among the inmate population. The jacket is also used as a smuggling tool. Some prisons do not allow the inmates to wear their jackets into the visiting room, however, that doesn't stop the drugs from coming in. The other sign of a mule is the inmates who are not wearing a belt. This informs other inmates that they are a mule. Visitors are instructed on how to package the drugs beforehand.

Drugs are packaged and wrapped in two different ways for different purposes. Some mules are willing to keister the drugs, inserted anally; other mules prefer to swallow small balloons filled with drugs that can be retrieved by vomiting once the mule leaves visiting.

The type of inmates who choose the swallowing method and refuse to keister are not considered mules. They don't offer their services to other inmates. They normally smuggle drugs in for themselves to use, sell, or both. The inmates who choose the swallowing method prepare themselves by drinking a few cups of water before going out to visit. Once he's in the visiting room, he will continue to drink liquids, usually water or fruit drinks, but not sodas because of the acid. The reason for this is because once he swallows the drugs, he can go right back to his cell and drink a few more cups of water and then force himself to vomit the drugs. The balloons float in the stomach and are easily retrieved. The inmate will have someone in the cell with him when he's extracting the drugs by vomiting. If a balloon gets caught in his throat, his friend can administer aid. If all the balloons don't come out, he would eat a can of chili beans or something heavy on the stomach to extract it through a bowel movement, but there's usually no problem getting all the balloons out by vomiting them.

The way the drugs are packaged for this method is by using small size balloons. The drugs are the stuffed into a small balloon just big enough to swallow. It is tied at the end and the extra is removed. It is repackaged into another small balloon, tied and the extra flap is removed. The double wrapping is a safety measure in case the first balloon should break inside the stomach, there would be another layer of protection.

The way that the drugs are packaged and wrapped for the mule who would be keistering them, they are compressed into a condom. The condom is tied and the excess is removed. Then it is wrapped in black or gray electric tape and then replaced into another condom or a large balloon that is tied on the end.

The inmates normally have a woman bring the drugs to them because women can hide the drugs on them without it being detected if they are asked to submit to a body or frisk search. The women are instructed to place the drugs in her vagina before coming into the prison for a visit. Additionally, they are instructed to wear a maxi pad so she can claim to be menstruating if asked to submit to a search. Once she's inside the visiting room, she will request to use the rest room. That's when she will remove the drugs from her vagina and place them in her bra underneath one of her breasts or in the front of her panties and return to the visiting room. She and the inmate would walk to the vending machine to purchase food items. Usually one of those items would be microwave popcorn. The inmate would stand blocking the view of the officers with his back toward them while his visitor is purchasing items. When she goes to remove the items from the machine, that's when she removes the drugs from her body and bring the food up with the drugs in her hand and then hands the drugs and the food to the inmate. They would then go to the microwave to pop the popcorn and warm other food items. If there is a small crowd of people standing in line waiting to use the microwave, the inmate would make his move keister the drugs standing up. One arm would be behind his back. His visitor would stand facing him blocking the view of the arm. If there is no one at the micro to block him, he would cook the microwave popcorn and place the drugs inside the bag, then they both would return to their seat. If the inmate is wearing a jacket, he would slide the arm that's not facing any officer out of the sleeve, scoot to the edge of his seat and slide his hands into his pants and keister the drugs from the front. Once the drugs are secured inside him, he can enjoy his visit. Now, if he's not wearing a jacket there are two main moves he would make. One, he would wait until count time when the inmates have to be counted and the officers' attention is focused on that, or he would wait until a few people go back to the microwave to cook food. He doesn't have to worry about the lubrication drying up because the popcorn will provide plenty.

The swallowers do not have to go through all the waits and changes once the drugs are inside the visiting room. His visitor places them in a bag of popcorn or potato chip bag and hand it to him. While the inmate eats the substance every now and then he can pop a balloon of drugs in his mouth and wash it down.

As for the inmates who have to visit behind the glass windows. The way they get their drugs is with the assistance of the inmate visiting room porter. The visitor comes in with the drugs, she buys herself some food items from the vending machine. She eats some of the items and places the drugs in the empty bag or food container. She then gives the porter a signal indicating that she's ready. He makes his way around toward her picking up trash. He removes the drugs and continues cleaning.

He then requests to use the inmate's restroom. When he uses the restroom, he leaves the drugs in the restroom trash can or in the paper towel dispenser. Once the porter returns back into the visiting room, the inmate behind the glass request to use the restroom, where he retrieves the drugs and keisters them. The porter would go pick up his issue after visiting is over. Usually it would be a quarter of whatever was brought in.

Every prison normally has a visiting room camera man who's usually an inmate. The cameraman is also the vehicle for smuggling drugs back into the prisons.

INSTITUTIONAL STAFF

In every prison there is someone of employment who is willing to smuggle in contraband for a reasonable fee. Either it's a correctional officer or a free staff who works at the prison, or both. It is common to find a correctional officer or free staff member working a side business with carefully screened inmates who are trusted to keep their mouths shut. These officers, staff members are direct and guaranteed vehicles for large amounts of drugs and contraband items, cellular phones, portable DVD players, handheld video games, bullets, pocket knives, food, shoes, porn magazines, handcuff keys, etc. The smugglers are paid in advance for their services with cash money.

The inmates also target female correctional officers to assist them in the trafficking. Their goal is to build an intimate relationship first, and once they do, that relationship becomes strictly about smuggling in contraband. The inmate would test the water by asking for items that seem harmless, like gum, food, lighters. Once the officer starts bringing in contraband, the inmate begins asking for bigger things. He would motivate her by promising or giving her a money gift. Many women correctional officers and staff members fall for this. Their greed for that extra few hundred dollars on top of their paycheck keeps them motivated. The relationship turns from intimate to nothing but business, just the way the inmate wanted from the start.

Prison gangs have particular members who are fast and slick talkers who they sic on correctional officers and staff members who seem to be easily manipulated for the very purpose of assisting the gang in drug trafficking. These inmates are given the permission to be in the police face constantly for that very purpose.

MAIL

Mail is another common way drugs and cash money are gotten into the prisons, although by using the mail to smuggle in drugs limits the quantity greatly. Here you will learn the methods of how drugs are sent into the institution via mail.

GREETING CARDS

Yes, greeting cards are the transporter of drugs and money. What other way to put a smile on a prisoner's face. The correspondents purchase cards that are made out of heavy card stock. Usually these types of cards have third flaps that are folded inward and factory glued to the inside around the edges. The correspondent lays the card on a flat surface and places a bandanna or some type of thin cloth over the card. A hot iron is run over the third flap. The iron is set on steam and the steam loosens the glue of the card. The card flap is then opened.

There are certain ways that drugs are placed in the card. Heroin, a strip of scotch tape is folded evenly longitudinally just enough to form a crease in the tape. It's then reopened and the Heroin is placed on the tape and the tape is folded over the heroin and sealed. The heroin is smashed down to even out the heroin. The tape is then carefully placed around the edges of the card flap. The flap is glued back and sealed back together. If correctly done, the card will not appear to have been tampered with. The money is sent by ironing it out to a crisp and taped flat inside the card and the flap is resealed.

METHAMPHETAMINE

The method for smuggling in this drug through the mail is a lot simpler than heroin. You could use any type of greeting card, heavy or light stock wouldn't matter. Why? Because there is no hiding involved, it is sent in where it could be noticed only by a pair of trained eyes. How? The methamphetamine is liquefied and poured onto the inside surface of the card and left to do dry by refrigerator. What happen is the drugs are on the paper.

If one were to look closely at the card surface they would notice a crystal sparkling effect almost like glitter. If the drug is not of a good quality it would turn the card stock a darker shade of its original color. That's why when methamphetamine is brushed, immersed or poured onto a greeting card, the correspondent selects a card with a color tone that the mark of the drug wouldn't be noticeable.

CHAPTER 2

ALCOHOL MANUFACTURING

Prisoners manufacture their own alcohol on a constant basis. It's a big commodity and financially profitable. In this chapter you will learn the basics on how prisoners make alcohol. Please note: The author or publisher holds no responsibility for anyone who chooses to prepare the alcohol. The information is to inform the reader on how prison alcohol is made; not for the sole purpose of preparing and consuming.

Prison made alcohol is prepared in many ways with different types of ingredients. The following ingredients are the products that are available to the prisoners on a daily basis or easily obtained. There are two different types of alcohol prisoners make. Pruno and white lightning, Pruno is Wine and in order to make white lightning you first have to make Pruno, because lightning is created from Pruno. White lightning is the strongest alcohol you can make in prison. It is clear, just like water, but has a kick like a bull. Every race has a professional wine maker who sells the liquid by the cups. The wine maker sets his own prices on what he wants to charge. The better the wine, the more you pay. The usual price ranges from $3 to $5 for a cup of pruno. White lightning is a lot more expensive and a cup of it could range from $15 to $25 dollars.

WINE (PRUNO)

Before the wine is made you first need a kicker. A kicker is what gets the wine to start cooking. If the wine maker works without a kicker he will not be able to make the wine. A kicker takes up to one week to make. Once you have a kicker you can continuously use it every time you decide to make a batch of wine. The more you use the kicker, the better the wine will turn out.

Kicker

2 cup fruit cocktail with liquid
1 potato diced
2 slices of bread
Preparation: mix ingredients together and place in a jar or cup with lid. Allow to ferment undisturbed for one week. Now you are ready to make wine.

The Wine

25 Apples
2 kool aid packages (16 oz. each) or sugar
4 cup hot water (16 oz. each)

Preparation: The apples are placed in a large plastic bag, then mashed up, then placed inside a sock. The juice is extracted from the apples by twisting the sock. Once all the apples are extracted of their juice, the leftover pulp is discarded and the juice is then placed in another plastic bag along with the kicker, the four cups of hot water and one of the kool aid packs or sugar is added and the bag is tied. The bag is wrapped in a blanket to add heat and placed somewhere safe to start cooking. Once the wine starts cooking, gasses will form and it would have to be burped to release them. Every so often because the bag will expand. The second day the other 16 oz. of kool Aid or sugar is added to the bag. The sugar will cook off.

How to tell when the wine is ready by taking a taste test? If the wine has a sweet taste, then it's not through cooking, but if it's a bitter taste, then it's ready. The wine is then drained through a sheet or a shirt and the leftover pulp is saved as the kicker for the next batch.

WHITE LIGHTNING (LIQUID CRACK)

White lightning is made from the wine (Pruno). The wine is placed in a hot pot. A small plastic bag is taped around the hot pot's rim to keep any air from escaping. A small size whole is placed in the corner of the bag and it is tilted directly over a bowl or large cup. The hot pot is turned on. What happens is that the wine is cooking and the steam is caught in the bag creating a mist. The liquid from steam will drizzle through the whole. That liquid is the alcohol, White Lightning.

PRISON SECRETS
Eugene L. Weems

CHAPTER 3

WEAPON MANUFACTURING

Prison-made weapons are manufactured out of just about any type of material you could possibly imagine. Here you will learn how some of the basic prison weapons are made.

Personal Identification

The prison ID card is made into a weapon when there are no other materials available to construct one. At some prisons they issue inmates hard plastic IDs while others issue the regular driver license type ID, the laminated soft plastic one. Either of the two works. One end of the widest side is sharpened into a sharp blade by sliding the card back and forth on a smooth concrete floor. Once it has a sharpness to it, rub soap on the end of it and let it dry. It would cut like a razor blade and the guards would never realize that an inmate has a weapon because all he sees is identification.

Pocket Comb

This is a very fast weapon to make and to the untrained eye it would go undetected. This weapon is used for slashing. A small pocket comb and one razor blade is all that it takes to make this weapon. The razor blade is removed from its holder and placed between two of the combs teeth to keep it in place and secured. The blade would be protruding from the comb teeth only slightly. The weapon is camouflage by placing the comb in the hair or holding it with your fingers over the end with the blade, or placed in their pocket.

Top Ramen Soup

I know you may be wondering how a weapon is made out of a soup. Well I will tell you. This is a weapon that is called a one hitter quitter neck shot. The Top Ramen noodle soup is cooked without breaking up the noodles leaving them long. They are cooked long enough just so they would unravel. They are laid out on the floor and then braided gently together. They are then left out until they are completely dried. Honey or table syrup is rubbed over the entire dried noodle and it is left out until it is dried.

Plastic Spoons

Two plastic spoons are placed together and tied with a piece of string, sheet or taped at the middle and wide end. Then the ends are sharpened to a fine point

Break offs

These knives fit their name because they're designed to be broken off inside a person. They are made out of the hard plastic tape cassette covers or hard plastic cups or plastic trays that the prisons serve the meals on. Some prisoners like designing nice looking knives so they will cut out a model of the shape of the knife they want out of a cardboard box. It is taped to the floor. They need fire for this process so usually they make a bong. A prison bong is toilet paper that is rolled over your hand six times or more, then tucked inside out. It should resemble a cone, mountain shape. It is placed on the edge of the stainless steel toilet seat and lit at the top. The bong would burn slowly, and it doesn't create any smoke.

Cassette Tape Covers

Use two cassette tape covers. Pour some baby oil on the floor. To start the melting process, let the cassette melt, then once it's soft scoop it onto the design model. Make the middle part of the knife thinner so once someone is stabbed with it, lift up and it would break off inside them. This same process is used with the plastic cups and trays. It is also used to make regular knives and when a knife is made out of plastic and then sharpened it is more dangerous than steel.

Bone Crushers

Bone crushers are knives made out of steel. Prisoners can get steel just about anywhere in the prisons. They take the metal from a desk or bunk bed in their cell, the kitchen, cookie sheets, from the inside of a typewriter, the bottom of hot pots, and more. Prisoners cut knives from the above mention items. How, you are wondering? Easily, all it takes is a pair of toenail clippers and some elbow grease and a little time. Prisoners would break the toe nail clippers in half, draw out there design of the knife on steel and use the pieces of the toe nail clipper to cut out the shape. Once it is cut out, then a handle is made out of cloth and it is sharpened on the ground or the side of the steel toilet. Steel sharpens steel.

Ice Picks

These are made from rods that are inside of typewriters, bed spring, fence, mop bucket and paint bucket handles etcetera. The tip is sharpened on concrete. A handle is made out of melted plastic tape or cloth. This weapon is one of the favorites to a lot of prisoners because once they stab someone with it, it does not leave a big bloody mess and it's easy to get rid of just by removing the handle and flushing the rest down the toilet. Most prisoners now prefer plastic knives over steel because they can't be detected by metal detectors, which allow them to keep the weapon in their cells and on them at all times.

The Places Knives Are Hidden:

Knives are hidden on the yards around the area of where groups work out or normally hang out. The weapons are usually placed inside the ground. They are also hidden in the units and the bottom of the garbage cans. The inmate unit porters are the ones who provide this hiding place for their gang and keep watch over it to make sure no other inmates go probing inside the garbage can.

The cells are a common place weapons are kept. They are hidden inside the appliance, (television, typewriters, radios), Inside the mattresses, pillows and inside the toilets. How the toilets, you are wondering? A shoe string or some type of string is tied on the knife. The other end is tied to a palm comb or a small comb. The knife is placed inside the drain of the toilet and the comb is bent inwardly and inserted into the hole so it would fit snuggly against its walls of the hole. This gives the illusion that nothing is inside the toilet and it will go unnoticed by untrained eyes who don't know what they are looking for.

There are other ways weapons are manufactured and places they are hidden. In this book I only provided you with the major information to the basics and the norm to the hiding spots that cover all prisons.

PRISON SECRETS
Eugene L. Weems

CHAPTER 4

PRISON RAPE

Prison rape does not happen as often as people think and it's not how the movies portray it to be. Please don't let me mislead you. Rape is a prisoner's reality and it does occur in different sensitive circumstances.

BOOTY BANDITS

Inmates who are into homosexual activities and lurk for new victims to have sex with are identified as booty bandits. These are the ones who lurk in silent shadows for the first timers and the young teenagers who come into the prisons, the ones who are easily intimidated, persuaded, influenced, weak, friendly or have feminine ways.

These booty bandits lure their victims with kindness, friendship, protection and a false illusion of caring. The booty bandit would start offering gifts or the use of his property, such as TV, Radio, books, clothes, food, hygiene, drugs, etcetera. Once his victim becomes indebted to the booty bandit, the booty bandit would normally try to get his victim moved into his cell so he could have the full range of dominating his prey mentally and physically without any interruption.

When gifts start being accepted, then that's when the booty bandit will show his true face from behind the deceitful mask he displays. He would start closing in on his prey with indirect statements about sex and sex playing, he becomes touchy, feely in a playful manner. All he's doing is testing the water to see how his victim is going to respond to his acts. If his victim doesn't react, then he knows he can make his move, but if his victim shows aggression, then he knows his approach would now have to be aggressive, and that's when the words "you owe me" comes into the picture.

His victim would be lured into a cell from viewing eyes and then spring his sexual request on his victim. If the victim refuses, then that's when the booty bandit tells him he owes him and wants to be paid with the same exact items he gave him. There's no possible way that the victim would be able to pay him with the exact items, maybe similar ones, but not the exact. The booty bandit knows that, which is his whole reason for requesting the exact items. This becomes the booty bandit's foundation to stand on as the excuse to do anything he decides to do to his victim by physical force. The booty bandit would become violent and threaten to kill his victim if he can't get his exact items. The victim would then usually submit to his requested sex act out of fear for his life, or if he stands his ground, that's when the booty bandit will try and take it by force. If he can't, then he would end up stabbing his victim, not over the gift he gave his victim, but out of anger that his plan didn't work. Normally, other prisoners do not get involved or question the booty bandit about him trying to sexually assault his victim because the booty bandit going to use the excuse that his victim owes him.

Then you have those booty bandits that would just knock you out and rape you without being bothered with all the pampering and delicate manipulation of luring his victim in.

GANG RAPE

Gang rape is very seldom heard of. This is something the movies would portray to the public, but in prisons you don't hear much about gang rapes. There might be a situation where several prisoners indulge in sexual acts with a homosexual or a prisoner who agreed to have sex with them for drugs or to clear up a debt, etcetera. Then once the act is over the person might of felt disrespected or didn't get what he was promised, so then he runs to the police and hollers he was gang raped. But other than that, it is very unlikely that you would hear about an inmate being gang raped. It just doesn't go down like the movies portray it.

RAPE

It happens inside the prisons normally with weak cell mates and cell mates who indulge in a lot of drugs (methamphetamine or cocaine). Prisoners who are rape victims usually don't tell anyone about it. It remains a secret with them to avoid the embarrassment and being humiliated and victimized by other prisoners. This activity normally occurs within the white race.

CHAPTER 5

PRISON RECIPES

The following recipes are the favorites of the prison population, which are prepared on a constant basis by those who have the means to do so. You will learn the ingredients, measurements and the procedures that is required to preparing the following prison dishes better known as (spreads). You will also learn the techniques to how they make candy, granola bars, and prison cheese. "Please note: The author or publisher holds no responsibility for those who choose to venture in preparing any of these recipes. The author's sole purpose was to provide information for the reader's edification, not for preparing and consuming.

Some of the ingredients you will read about in the recipes are obtained from the daily meals and sack lunches that are provided by the prison. The items change daily that are contained inside the lunches, but mainly it consist of the following items: apple or orange, pack of bread that contains four individual slices, pack of meat with two thin slices of either bologna, salami or mystery meat. Mystery meat is a mystery because some of the meats have thin slices of jalapeños embedded into them. Some come with two different shades of color light pinkish on one half of a side and it fades into a darker color that resembles a bruise. The other type comes in a dark reddish color with black speckles of spices.

Some days other than getting meat there would be a substitute of a 2-ounce pack of peanut butter and a 1-ounce pack of jelly, a cookie, and 1-ounce bag of seeds, nuts, gram crackers or dried fruits. 1 pack of instant kool aid that makes one cup, 2-ounce bag of chips or pretzels, mustard, mayonnaise, relish condiments. The other items are purchased from the prison canteen or, if not available out of the canteen, are stolen from the prison kitchen.

Poor Man's spread

This meal is identified as a poor man's spread because of the small number of items it takes to make. The majority of the inmates prepare it or something similar.

Prep time: 5 minutes
Servings: 1
1 package Top Ramen soup
1 mustard pack
Preparation: Cook the noodles until they begin to soften, drain the excess water. Add the seasoning pack and remaining ingredients mix it up and it's ready to eat.

Prison Spread

This meal is called the prison spread for a reason. It's the top spread of all spreads exceptional to the gumbo spread. Inmates indulge themselves in preparing and consuming this meal regularly.

Prep time: 10 minutes
Servings 2 hungry people
3 packages Top Ramen soup (your choice of flavor)
1 summer sausage (8 oz.) diced
4 oz. Instant refried beans
3 tbsp. jalapeno cheese spread
1 tablespoon of mayonnaise
1 bag of 5 oz. hot 8 spicy pork skins
1 bag (3.25 oz.) chili cheese Fritos.
Preparation: Bring water to a boil and add the noodles, summer sausage and refried beans together. Cook until the noodles begin to soften. Drain most of

the remaining water. Add all ingredients into a durable plastic bag, mix well. Let it sit for two minutes until noodles soften and soak up seasoning and water.

Prison Gumbo

This spread is considered a delicacy for it is prepared only on special occasions because it is a very expensive meal to prepare and an inmate could eat for two months for what it cost to make the meal.

Prep time: 30 minuets

8 seasoning packs from a beef flavor Top Ramen soup

1 box of Minute Rice (14 oz.)

1 cup whole Kernel of Corn

3 Summer Sausages (8 oz. each) Sliced 1/8 inch thick

1 bag Teriyaki beef Jerk (4 oz. shredded)

2 Pouches of Chicken (3.25 oz. each)

2 Pouches of oysters (3.25 oz. each)

1 Package of Squid (4 0z)

2 Pouches Crabmeat (3.25 oz.)

2 cup Okra Pods diced

Preparation: Bring the water to a boil. Add the okra, corn, seasoning pack, squid, chicken, crab meat, summer sausage and simmer for 20 minutes, stirring occasionally. Then add shrimp, beef jerky, oysters and simmer for 5 minutes. Cook the rice separately.

Candy

There are several different flavors that could be made with the replacement of the flavored ingredients.

Prep time: 36 hours
1 grape jelly 12 oz. or your flavor choice
1 package of grape Kool Aid 2 oz.
Preparation: Squeeze the jelly into a small plastic bag. Add half the pack of Kool Aid and mix the two by using the outside of the bag continue to add Kool Aid until the jelly starts to form into thick dough. Then shape the contents into your desired shape and lay them out on a new piece of plastic in the open until they harden.

Granola Bar

This is a tasty snack and a good commodity for hustlers to sell to their individual race. The races have rules not to purchase open food items from other races. The granola bars are normally sold two for one dollar.

Prep Time: 24 hours
Servings: 3
3 cups Kellogg's complete wheat bran flakes cereal
2 packs Peanut butter 2 oz. each
3 packs table syrup ½ oz. each
3 packs mix dried fruit 1 oz. each diced
3 packs almonds 10 oz. each
3 packs roasted peanuts 1 oz. each
8 gram crackers
Preparation: Put the cereal and gram crackers into a plastic bag and crush it up into small pieces. Add the

remaining ingredients and mix together. Then start forming your bars in your preferred shape and size. Then set them on a plate to harden.

Prison Cheese

Prison cheese is easy to make and tastes like cream cheese. It is a long process to prepare, but what is time to a prisoner? Cheese is usually made when an inmate is in confinement for discipline reasons. In preparing the cheese the smell can be overwhelming to a sensitive nose.

Prep time: One week
Servings: 2
1 milk ½ pint
1 seasoning pack from a chili top Ramen soup
Preparation: Place the milk in a place where it won't be disturbed. Do not open it or shake it up. Let it sit for six days. Then open it and drain the water from the carton carefully. Then sprinkle half the chili seasoning over the cheese let it sit for a few hours and drain the excess water off again. Place the cheese on a piece of plastic and sprinkle some more seasoning over it. Then let it sit out until the next day.

CHAPTER 6

MUSLIMS

"I thank you for taking the time to sit and do this interview with me. Can you give me a little history about what is a Muslim and their beliefs?"

First allow me to say "Assalamu Alaikum." I would like to begin this interview by opening up with the Al-Fatiha. In the name of Allah, most gracious, most merciful. Praise be to Allah, the cherisher and sustainer of the worlds; most gracious, most merciful; master of the Day of Judgment. You do we worship, and your aid do we seek. Show us the straightway, the way of those on whom you have bestowed your grace, those is not wrath, and who do not go astray.

A Muslim is a believer of one God who is Allah. Muslim male and female is obliged to offer the Lqamat-as-Salat; which means in Arabic language the performance of Salat (Prayers) is done regularly five times a day at the specified times the same way that the last prophet, Muhammad used to offer them, standing, bowing, prostrating, and sitting facing Mecca. In order for a person to become a Muslim, he must first take his Shahabad (confession). They must make an open confession by mouth and with their heart by quoting the following, "La ilaha illallah, Muhammad-ur-rasul-Allah," which means, "There is no God but Allah and Muhammad is his messenger."

A Muslim must follow the five principles of Islam, which are: (1) To testify that there is no God but Allah and Muhammad is his messenger. (2) To perform lqamat-as-salat, the five compulsory congregational prayers. (3) To pay zakat, a yearly fixed portion for the benefit of the poor in the Muslim community. (4) To perform Hajj, Pilgrimage to mecca. (5) To observe saum, fasting during the month of Ramadan every year, the holy month. And must believe in the six articles of faith. (1) Allah, (2) His Angels, (3), His messengers, (4) His revealed books, (5) The day of resurrection, (6) the divine preordainments that Allah has ordained (Al-Qador).

We follow the Sunnah, legal ways, orders, acts of worship of Allah's messenger and the last of all his prophets Muhammad (Subhanahu wa-ta-ala). The noble Quran is the book that was revealed to Prophet Muhammad of the laws decreed for mankind. The prophet was born 570 after Death and returned back to

Allah (Subhanahu-wa-ta-ala) in 632 after death. The Noble Quran has 114 suras (chapters), 6,236 Ayats (verses of revelations), and approximately 77,934 words, but it is said that if Allah was to reveal everything he wanted us to know that two seas of ink wouldn't be enough for his words. The greatest Surah in the Quran is the Al-Fatihah (the opening), the one I recited before we began this interview. It's mandatory that we recite it in our prayers or our prayers are no good.

"Are the Muslims inside the prisons a gang?"

Subhan Allah, we are a gang for Allah the most gracious, most merciful of the worlds. We are the biggest fraction in the prison systems, but we are not part of Shatan, the Devil human creations. We don't involve ourselves in Haram, unlawful and forbidden acts of our religion, Al-Islam. Islam means peace. We as Muslims must strive in the ways of Islam and not sinful ways of the world. The prisons try to label Muslims as a prison gang due to some new Muslims who backslide, losing focus of their Deem (religion) and fall prey back to their human ways and functions they were in involved in before they came to Islam. We must understand people always look for fault in what's good consciously or unconsciously. The administration of these institutions do so, as well.

Most Muslims who come to Islam in the prisons are ex-gang members who normally still have ties with their ex-gang. It is difficult for a person to cut all ties with the people they are familiar with, comfortable being around and who have long history together. It's also

73

difficult for a person to stop bad habits all at once. Change only comes with time, patience, consistency and the desire to do so.

"Are all Muslims in prison African American?"

Majority yes, but not all. There is a mixture of all races except whites. Not that whites are not welcome to Islam, but from the 40 years I've been in and out of prisons in eight different states, not once have I seen a white Muslim. I'm not claiming that there aren't any; I just don't know of any in the prisons.

"Do the Muslims get into prison riots?"

We prefer not to, but there are occasions when we must involve ourselves. Especially when a different race takes fight on anything that's African American. Other races don't see Muslims, they see a dark shade and that's who they attack. When their race decides they're going to war with a particular race, then that race is the enemy. There had been attacks on Muslims that way and we are not accepting those types of mistakes. We held jihad right on the spot against the race who assaulted our Muslim brother.

Let's not forget that there are Muslims who are pro black and militant, who is the Nation of Islam. Those are our Muslim brothers, but one thing for sure; if there is a threat or attack on the black race, they will involve themselves in the battle and that pulls the other Muslims in. It also causes problems among the community because some Muslims feel that all Muslims should be neutral when it comes to anything that has nothing to do with a Muslim, and that is where black Muslims are put in a catch twenty-two. For one thing, if a Muslim does decide he is not going to get involved with a race riot, but then he is attacked and stabbed or, let's just say killed, that makes it a Muslim community issue which we will have to face. The Quran tells us not to turn our backs on another Muslim but to fight to the death at his side, and that is how I move, and I move with my race being that if they see a Muslim getting attacked, you can believe the blacks are going to assist that Muslim. And like I said earlier, you have a lot of Muslims who are ex-gang members but still have love from that gang and when that ex-gang member gets involved into something, his ex-gang going to assist. That is just how it goes.

On different prison yards the Muslim community may function differently than other places. It all depends on the yard Imam, the Muslim's caliph (head person) who is also the one who leads us in the Salat (prayer) during services, and the Khalifah (leadership). They are the ones who set the rules for Muslims on the yard. I have seen when Muslims try to run a program that is not in agreement with the nation of Islam. They will branch off and be two separate communities.

"When other Muslims come into the prison system how are they treated?"

All our Muslim brothers are treated with the utmost respect and greeted with the Muslim blessings of Assalamu Alaikum. We furnish them with the necessities and provide a television or radio for entertainment. The Muslim personal library is always open to them to check out books or tapes. We have a designated Muslim who is our librarian.

"What about those who are not Muslims; can they come to the services?"

Yes and no. We invite guests to attend the services, but on the high security yards we only allow Muslims to attend due to safety reasons. We do try to bring others to Islam, especially the teens that come into the prisons. If we can get a hold of them before the gangs get a chance to corrupt their minds, then we do, but most of the time when a youth comes in, he's normally already part of a street gang and has homeboys on the yard and that's the crowd who he ends up functioning with.

"Are there any gays in the Muslim community?"

Subhan Allah, we do not allow homosexuals in Islam. That is a blasphemy to Allah and disrespect to Islam and all Muslims. We do not believe in homosexuality. I am surprised you would even ask such a disrespectful question. We do speak to the gays on the yard and give them respect, but coming to Islam is out of the question. It is just not going to happen.

"How do Muslims make money on the yards?"

We sell body and incense oils to the population. Incense oils sell for $4 to $5 for a quarter once, $6 to $8 for a half, and $10 to $12 for a full ounce. The body oils are twice as expensive.

We also have talents that we capitalize on. Muslims artists draw greeting cards and portraits. We have paralegals that assist prisoners with legal matters. We

76

have professional typist who type up documents, letters, legal briefs. We have business consultants who help prisoners' families with outside businesses. We have electricians who fix appliances. There is always someone among us who has a special skill in some area.

"How about drugs, do Muslims sell drugs?"

Yes, there are Muslims who sell drugs and smuggle them into the prison. Muslims who do this do it secretly so other Muslims can't know. They sell drugs for personal gain, not for the community. When this Muslim gets caught in the act, he is brought up on charges and we will excommunicate him. But two Muslims have to witness the fact that a Muslim is involved in wrongdoing that's against Islamic law. When a Muslim is excommunicated from the community, the other Muslims are not allowed to socialize or acknowledge his presence while he's excommunicated. This is a form of punishment.

Drugs inside the prison are a big business, bigger than on the streets. There is much money to be made and drugs allow a person to accumulate every luxury that is offered inside. It also gives a person power and a voice that would be heard. The drug addicts from the different races is not going to want their drug connection to be busted or placed in any position that would hinder him from being able to supply the drugs, so they will stand up for him against their race. Then you have the sidekicks, his runners, flunkies, protection crew, business associates who he looks out for, who provide them with the means to put food in their mouths and hygiene products to stay clean and smelling good. Who makes it possible for them to have some of the prison luxuries? These individuals will protect the one who's supporting them at any cost.

A lot of these guys who sell drugs on the yard support their families in society or take care of their girlfriends, providing the money for them to visit. So when you are dealing drugs and it's on a big scale, not only are you making a lot of money, but you are the doorway for others to make money as well. A lot of inmates don't have other means to obtain finances to support themselves other than selling drugs, so when a person or group tries to bring down the man, there will be physical violence. So the Muslims who do have their hands in the drug business, as long as they are not openly out with it so other Muslims can see what they are doing, then there shouldn't and won't be a problem, simple as that.

We know that many of the Muslims in prisons have yet to give up all their old habits. Allah sees everything they do and is patient, and knows that the flesh is weak and the soul is easily manipulated.

"Being that Muslims are not a gang, what gives you the authority to speak for Muslims?"

It's just like a Kafir (disbeliever) to ask such a question. For one, Muslims have only one leader and that is Allah. I represent for Allah. I am a kalinafah who is respected throughout the prisons in many different states. My actions, deeds and sacrifices for the Muslim communities give me the honor to address your questions directed toward Muslims, and on this yard I am the only one who's in the position to do so.

"Do the Muslims have a mandatory workout program?"

Of course we have a mandatory workout program. We believe in keeping the mind, body and soul in the best shape possible. Our workouts do not consist of only physical workouts. We have mental and spiritual workouts as well. We keep our minds strong, swift, alert and active by academic studies, acquiring as much knowledge as possible while learning to speak different languages. Our spiritual studies are from the Holy Quran in order to become oneness with Allah. The physical workouts consist of calisthenics, road work, and self-defense training conducted secretly. The Muslim community has a wide range of professional martial artists and each one teaches one.

"How do Muslims feel about the police?"

I am not able to answer that question for the entire community, for everyone has their own personal outlook and opinions about the police. As Muslims, we are obligated to be at our best in caricature, dress, manner, neatness and attitude. We are obligated to be righteous and respectful and to refrain from back biting, frivolous conversation and negative behavior. In order to do that, one must not harvest ill feelings toward anyone. The police have a job to do. They are under obligations to a duty just like Muslims and gang members are to their own group. Once a person understands that, then he would be able to deal with negative feelings toward a person or class of people. I view it this way: police must do what they have to and we must do the same. It's all even and fair. My feelings toward the police are the same as toward everyone else, humble.

"I thought all Muslims were militant and hostile."

That's where lack of knowledge hinders you. If a person's range of information is narrow, then how does he expect to grasp the understanding of things that are right before his eyes? I can't stress the fact enough that knowledge is power, more powerful than money. Education is the key to that knowledge. Muslims are taught discipline, humbleness, and to take the middle course to problems. We are hostile only in the eyes of the wicked, the real evil doers. The devil doesn't like to be stood up to and challenged with the same type of aggressive attacks he uses. We are instructed by Allah to fight to death, hold jihad. We are the Ghazi of Allah. If our lives are being threatened, then we will do whatever we must to protect Muslims regardless, Allahu-Akbar, Allahu-Akbar, and Allahu Akbar. God is most great.

"How do Muslims feel about men raping men?"

How are we supposed to feel? Muslims are conditioned to stay clear of such impure, wicked thoughts. Although rapes happen inside the prisons, we are not superheroes. We don't know when it's going to happen and we can't be there to save those who are about to become sexual assault victims. It doesn't sit well with us in any form or fashion. If we observe something like that about to go down, we will intervene and stop it no matter what race it is.

We are highly respected by all races and gangs on the yards. There is a universal understanding that if you do something to a Muslim, get prepared for a war. If the problem could be worked out verbally, then that's the course we will take and accept, but if not, we will not simply poke you a few times with a knife. We are coming with every intention to put you six feet deep. Regardless if the officers are watching or not, business is going to be taken care of accordingly, and if the officers get in the way, they will just become one of our victims also. In these prisons a Muslim does not ever have to worry about someone trying to rape him. If anyone is ever bold enough to cross that line, we will take his life. There will be no escape, no running to prison cops. We always have Ghazis ready to take care of Muslim business.

In the prison we run a tight program. We try to keep to Muslim business only unless a matter pops up that affects the entire population; then we will investigate. This prison life is a very inhuman place to be. There's nothing here but a lot of sadness, misery, hatred, violence and a monotonous rotation of frustration, deception and distress, and death for those who lose hope and become a slave to the lifestyle. I see inmates on a daily bases chasing dope or drink, anything to stay intoxicated to escape this place. That's one of the reasons why drugs are at such a high demand and inmates will pay just about any price. A heroin addict would sell his soul for a fix, if he could. This is hell on earth because I see the devil and his demons every day that I awake.

CHAPTER 7

NAZI LOW RIDERS -- NLR

"What are Nazi Low Riders?" I asked.

Nazi Low Riders are not necessarily white boys. We are a mixture! We are part white, part Mexican, part Asian and part Indian. What we are supposed to be are individuals whose heart is white, down for the white race. We are the cream of the crop with gangster-like mentalities. We started off as hard core white boys with hearts of a lion, a Cholo likeness in dress, and Gangster Nazis, to be precise.

"Tell me when the NLR began and how the name came about?"

In the late seventies we got started up in the Northern Youth Authorities, Preston Penitentiary. Twelve white boys with the folio criteria who use to ride with the Surenos when it would jump with the northerners. A South Sider started calling us the Nazi Low Riders. It was just a nickname meant in good humor, but became a nightmare for many.

"What do the NLR stand for?"

We represent white power. For many, National Socialism, but in reality we are just a bunch of vipers waiting to unleash our poisonous venom into the mainstream prison life, to wreak havoc and instill fear among those who are beneath us. Who are beneath us? Anyone not behind the vicious number 44. Our numbers were kept to a selective few, only the strongest. We were the knights in shining armor among our own race, Captain Save-a-Wood!

Then in the mid nineties we were given the green light by our forefathers (The Brand) Aryan Brotherhood to graduate from Youth Authority to the state pen under the stipulation that we were to be their arms and legs. Their Torpedoes. We were to be their training ground. Once we climbed the ladder, our next step or phase was to graduate once again and become one of them, an Aryan Brother. But being our numbers were so few, we began a top level massive recruitment.

Our first and most costly mistake was when one Skinhead became envious because a lot of them had joined our numbers, causing their comrades to strongly dislike us. Additionally, we took down anyone in our path. Anyone not submitting to our reign, they had to bow down and kiss my ring or pay the penalty. Our mentalities are so wicked we did not hesitate to break all resistance. What started as a mighty force for building our race became a modern day SS Gestapo force that wrecked many good white men. We got too big too fast with no chain of command for guidelines.

In having this dominant way of thinking, we alienate our own races and caused separatism among a race whose strength was not up to par with other races, weakening our fold and not strengthening. Although the Skins and the Woods never had the courage to step up and check our momentum, their dislike and hatred toward us was evident, but we still held the keys every place we were present. Every prison yard belonged to the Riders. No Questions Asked.

"How can a Wood become a Nazi Low Rider?"

Back in Youth Authority you got jumped in, but as we grew and became who we are today, we wanted killers and not just averagely down white boys. So you had to book (stab) your way in! Whether you are a rat, child molester, Jew or a black, blood on a knife was the way to get in. Once you got in, you earned your bones. You could not just get the letters N L R tattooed on you. You had to earn each letter with the shed of blood. Earn your colors or earn your letters both mean the same.

Once our unquestionable dominance was law, we began to check every person (white) who stepped on our yards. Mandatory paperwork but not as thoroughly as we did in the Ad-Seg or SHU. In the lockdown units, we need to see your 114 lockup order and every classification chronological as well, but out on the yards was more by word of mouth. If somebody recognized a rat, Chester, they either produced paperwork or handled it.

Another mistake of ours was our favoritism. If a comrade fellow Rider said it was so, then we acted upon his word and putt holes. This was not good due to personal beefs, but we were Riders. No slipping, no sliding, just Nazi Low Riding. 44 is our gang number. The Wood Pile has a number 23, meaning the 23rd letter of the alphabet is "W" that stands for White or Wood. Skinheads have the number 88. The 8th letter of the alphabet is "H" so 88 equal HH equal Hail Hitler. So the Riders have the number 44. "N" is the 14th letter of the alphabet, "L" is the 12th letter and "R" is the 18th letter, so 14+12+18=44 and 44 equal NLR.

The COs in many prisons would give us the low down on many child molesters and turned their backs as blood flowed. They knew we weren't hesitating to probe a Chester's body with holes.

"How do the NLR make money inside the prison?"

Every white man who has the courage to step foot into our domain with a *clavo*, a lump of dope, has to break ours off, pay rent or give us 1/3 of their shit or get it taken with a lot of hurting. If a Low Rider went to store and did not contribute to the Rider's kitty, a collection given to the Riders who care to portion out to whites who did not get store, he got dealt with severely. Usually it's 20 percent that is recommended to be contributed. But most Riders raped the kitty and dared to be questioned on it. The funniest part of it all is, for the most part there are no set rules with the exception of one: Riders are right depending on what institute you are at and who's running the show and what Riders are there. For the most part it was all about the Riders coming up at everyone else's peril. We are plotters and planners. We plot against and are brave enough to go against the grain. We set into motion it was all about do everything for the Riders and don't ever go against it.

"What is it like to be a shot caller for the NLR?"

Holding the keys for the ride is like walking into a snake pit. You have to be on your toes and stay ahead of the snakes. It is more deadly and hazardous to my health than going to war with another race. No matter how strong or how much of the game you know eventually you are going to get holes put in you. If not, you definitely are not a strong individual and are doing something wrong. That's the sickness of it all. That's why we are sick ass Nazis. We have a thirst for violence just like a pit bull. That first taste of blood is all it takes for the demons to take over, and I'm a lot worse than most. See, as the shot caller you have envious eyes on you with a hunger for your shoes. It's called the balance of power. One minute you hold the power, the next you're leaking from newly acquired holes. Some last longer than others, but it's inevitable that you meet your demise sooner or later. Mine just hasn't come yet, but the rush, the thrill of having so much ruthless hatred at your disposal and being able to put a leash on your dogs of war or unleashing them to wreak havoc and chaos with the snap of a finger is such adrenaline rush, and they are in action without a first thought, the twisted mentality of an insane mind seeking death. Staying in power knowing it's only a matter of time, watching the mask being put on the falseness of their professions of love and honor and loyalty to a cause that is nonexistent. The genuine courage and strength it takes to play in this playground for periods at a time is great.

They say you tell a man's strength by the strength of his enemies. I am here to verify the truth to that. The more enemies you have and to what level of power they hold shines ten times on you as being that much more. To face the false fronts that your enemies put up knowing it's coming and their eyes are stoking you, waiting for you to slip up, patiently planning and plotting. Knowing it is going to happen but facing it as everyday life. I am not meaning to paint the picture that all comrades are demons; they are just all vipers.

"So there are rules for the Nazi Low Riders?"

The prisons labeled us a prison gang, and in truth, technically we are but structurally we are far from it. The closest thing we have to structure is our churches in Ad-Seg, SHU, and even mainline yards. We have meetings and vote for what actions we deem appropriate. This action was more prominent in Youth Authority and in the beginning stages of our stepping into the big house. As the later stages came it was more a front, a way of pacifying the Low Riders into feeling special and a part of something important, but when all is said and done, the key holder made the calls.

We don't force membership on anyone. On the contrary, we pick and choose our members; some for selfish reasons, some for loneliness, but we pick you, not you us and for the most part it's not just any old body. You have to have heart or at least act like you do. But in the same sense, a lot of Riders abuse the recruitment and are allowed walk in, not blooded in. Not just any old Wood will be elected to step up, and if we choose someone but they don't want to, that's fine, but not once have I witnessed a refusal in the 28 years that I have been riding.

A lot of our ranks come from who we considered our ill brothers, Skinheads. They felt that being fellow Nazis they should be equal to us. What a joke! We've gone to war and put down their ill rebellions numerous times, creating a deeper felt hatred among us. My personal feelings were that we were kinfolk, but that was never adopted. NLR and Skinheads started off as fellow Nazis comrades, but envy on their side and power on ours drove a wedge between us. To us, Skins are nothing more than our servants, peasants to serve us as we deem fit. As for the regular Woods nothing more than lames, prey for us predators. Once in a great while we find one with admirable qualities, one that shines above the crowd. They are snatched up, recruited into one of us. Other than that, the rest were expendable.

"Does the NLR have a mandatory workout program like other gangs do?"

A few of us are into building ourselves mentally, physically and spiritually. Not the religion aspects but our soul, strong inside and out. Not so much on mainline but in the Ad-Seg and SHUs, no excuses; you did it or got regulated. The workout varied from one place to the next, but basically consisted of burpies for strength and wind. Whoever ran the routine would say "down." The rest would go down and come up with a loud "one." We did a cadence when we came to our "four" we said "Thor God of war" as silly as it sounds being Thor was not the God of war. We just said it anyway for the rhyme and it was a mental psyche-out. For the six we said "sick ass Nazi." Eights were "hate" with anywhere from five to twenty-five Riders all sounding off at the same time. You can imagine the adrenaline rush and how pumped up you become.

Now let me digress back for a moment to answer your question as to how we make money in the prisons. It's not so much us making money, more like extorting money by pressuring other whites. We do fairly well. If you don't freely relinquish what we request, you get hurt with the loss of it all. Most are smart enough to ask us what we need without us approaching them.

"What does the lightning bolt tattoo mean?"

The double lightning bolt preferable on the inside of our bicep usually meant you stabbed a nigger. It used to be honored, but with the way prisons are now, anybody could buy a tattoo without earning or even knowing the significance of its true value. That's why a lot of us do not wear the easily bought stripes. The swastika represents the same and the devaluing of its meaning has met the same downfall as the SS bolts. Double lightning bolts come from World War II, Nazi Germany, but again the Swastika or Swazi and bolts basically have no true meaning. They are just a commercial tattoo these days.

The cadence that was spoken about earlier, our motto is, "No slipping, no sliding, just Nazi Low Riding." Our song is an oldie. All my friends are Low Riders, but we just add Nazi before Low Riders.

As for our structure, here is a prime example of our lack of structure. We claim to be white power, but we have Asian/Caucasian, Mexican/Caucasian and Indian/Caucasian, and we even have a pure Indian that's a NLR, but they claim and ride under white power. Those that are mix breeds disown the other part of their heritage and accept the white side of them as their true and only heritage. So how can we be fully racial? What we are is simple. For the most part, are the definition of German, which is "War men." We are blood lusting convicts who thrive off of violence. If we aren't at war with somebody, we get bored and start one. We claim to hate Niggers, kikes and northern Mexicans, and the Asians are borderline. For the most part, as long as it suits our needs, we deal with them on a mutual respect level, but you will never see us accepting any open food items or tobacco products from them. You will never catch us eating, drinking, and smoking behind them, or sitting at the same tables. That protocol is the way prison unwritten law has been for cons and as with those before us. We just followed suit and respect the ways of our forefathers, plus it fits into The Nazi Low Rider mentality of hate. We hate everyone and everything not with us and even some that are. It's all an excuse to start

91

something violent for our pleasure and excitement. That's the only way I know how to put it.

"Is the NLR into gang raping other prisoners?"

People have misconceptions about the prison life about people getting raped. For the NLR that is purely fictitious and is so far from the truth when it comes to the Riders. First, there are so many homosexuals, nobody needs to rape anyone. It happens with other groups, but not with the Riders. We don't get into other's business so I will not speak on that subject. You are right here in prison with me and know the people to get at about that. The NLR is not one of them.

"Who does the NLR stay at war with?"

We stay at war with the Niggers, but we have been to war with every faction. Niggers, Nips, busters, sewer rats, Skins, Woods, brand, Mexican mafia, Northerners, Kikes are just victimized. No heart, no back bone, just weak.

"Does the NLR really like the Southern Mexicans?"

Us and Southern Mexicans use to be tight, but even though we roll with each other once in a while just for history sake, we don't care for them. We consider them bean pushing, taco bending straight hair niggers with light skin, not to be trusted a branch of the mud race.

"Do the Nazi Low Riders use drugs?"

Of course we get high. Some like tar, white girl, but most like white sinister. We dip and dabble in every drug. But the most favorite among my race is tar and white sinister, better known as crystal meth.

My deepest personal outlook of a family I have dedicated 28 years of my life to what people need to know is that no matter how structured a group may seem, there is always a flip side to every story. Nazi Low Rider is an oxymoron from its name to everything we turned out to be. Its only loyalty is to its members, and that's 100 percent true and real from a warrior who is every bit a Nazi Low Rider.

PRISON SECRETS
Eugene L. Weems

CHAPTER 8

GAY BOY GANGSTER -- GBG

"What is a Gay Boy Gangster?" I asked.

He, who likes to be identified as a she, sat in silence for a few minutes looking up at me. She had a cunning smirk, deliberately prolonging the interview. I had assumed he was admiring my handsomeness and being flirtatious how he bit on his bottom lips, staring with lustful eyes before he spoke with a gentle soft voice that didn't cognate with his actual gender, but it did match his altered appearance.

Well, I am going to break it all down plain and simple for you about us homosexuals who love dick. Big thick ones preferably. Everyone in the world already knows what homosexuals like, to suck and get fucked, but some of us also like to give it than receiving it all the time, and yes, I am one of those. I am into role playing; some days I like being the top and other days the bottom. I know you probably don't know what that mean since you don't indulge in such overwhelming, mind blowing, physical sexual pleasures, to a deep spiral of sensation, an unspoken intimacy of sensuality of the erotic. The top is a person who does the fucking in his lover's ass and the bottom is the one who gets fucked, which I don't think of my butt as that. I call my butt a pussy because I can work it better than any woman can; make you say things you never thought you would say.

"How about we move on to another subject like telling me about your gang?"

I am one of the founders of the secret society homosexual gang known as the Gay Boy Gangsters. We are not like other gangs; I want to make that clear. We are not boastful in advertising our gang name. We are not into the criminal violent activities or harming people. We are about making money and supporting each other, mentally, spiritually, physically and sexually if need be. A few friends and I started this gang so other homosexuals like ourselves would have a solid foundation to a support system and protection from the gay bashers and any others who felt the need to be violent toward us. We originally started on the streets of Los Angeles California when a lot of homosexuals were hustling the downtown and Hollywood area on Sunset before we started getting busted for selling drugs, prostitution, boosting, identity theft, forgery and credit card fraud and being sent to the pen. Some of my dawns were on probation and parole from different states and were expedited to their state for parole violation.

We had never expected for GBG to migrate as it has to other states and prisons around the world. I know some of my dawns were in prisons in different states who had recruited more members, but that is to be expected from any one of us wherever we went. We have to establish that support system wherever we go.

"How about telling me what it is like for a gay inside the prison?"

Most of the time it's exciting because you are around so many men and get to see big cocks and tight ass cheeks. It is wonderful. But it is not always smiles and high spirits. Some prisons the inmates do not allow homosexuals to walk the yard. As soon as one of my kind hit the yard, he's rushed by his race. Let me just say this so I can make it clear for you. Please don't get the wrong impression about us, because we chose to be the way that we are. That doesn't make us weak or pushovers. A lot of us have major chukkas and don't have a problem throwing them from the shoulders or slashing or running a long piece of steel in a mother fucker. A lot of men in the prison get us misconstrued and feel they can talk to us any old kind of way or lay hand down, but the reality of it is that we are still men with dicks who would get off in that ass more than just sexually. I do not like to lose sight of my femininity, but I will in order to protect myself or one of my members. We can be aggressive and get down with the get down also. I have been there and done that many of times, drain a few souls from their bodies for playing me too close. That's why I have a life sentence right now. I hate to think about it, but I picked all that time up right here in prison when I only had a one year parole violation from the start. Now look at me; I am doing life and do not have to get back.

You know what, though, and I raise my right hand up to God to what I am about to say, so helped me God or stick me dead. Most of the men in prison who talk negative about homosexuals, who frown up at our sight or have some type of dislike about us for whatever it may be, they are the ones who are really curious about our lifestyle. They are overt admirers and some of our biggest fans. I have exploited and seduced many of men who, quote/unquote, are supposed to be heterosexual. I am not talking about the men on the streets; I am referring to the so-called hard, though guys, gangsters and killers inside these prisons who frown up at the sight of my kind when they are in the presence of their friends but smile at us when they think the coast is clear of watchful eyes. A lot of these guys proposition us with canteen and drugs for sexual favors, always talking about keep it on the down.

But they are not the only ones. It is not unusual for a correctional officer to make sexual advances or propositions. I have had my share of turning dates with a few different correctional officers who paid me handsomely for a blow job or just to suck me off. We do take full advantage of those types of tricks. We make their asses pay swell and continuously for helping to fulfill their freakish fetish. They become our mule who smuggle drugs, panties, makeup, food, cell phones and whatever else we might need or want. If they refuse to do it, which 99% of the time they don't, we will holler rape, sexual assault and the correctional officer do not want that, because a lot of them have a wife and family and they don't want to be put in a position of being humiliated in front of their peers and in the public eyes so they just kick out like we ask.

The inmates are a little different. You can't just threaten them like that because some don't care if you go tell or not, but if he is a part of a gang, then he has to worry because they will do him in. The problem with that is that the one you tell on most likely will try to kill you before his gang gets a chance to get him, so we have to be careful how we approach situations like that. We do have a way for handling inmate tricks. When one of them request for us to sneak over to their cell for sex, we charge them, we stay manipulating. I been with men who gotten sprung on the pussy who broke ties with wives because they wanted to be with me. I had some become extremely jealous and overly aggressive about me socializing with someone else. I even received marriage proposals. It is crazy how this prison life is a world within a world where there is no limitation to the criminal imagination. It is likes some strong and weird provocative shit that's going on in these stoops. I have witnessed in the privacy of a cell some of the hard core, thuggish, and heartless criminals turn bitch during our sexual acts, allowing themselves to be free to the pleasures of my love making, giving me a reach-around as they pump inside of my pussy doggy style. Some even requested that I fuck them in the ass. Oh yes, believe it honey, this is how it goes down in prison. You ask me to give you the real for your book and I am giving it to you without pulling any punches. The women out there in the world need to know about some of these men in these prisons who are claiming to be all man and strictly on pussy. That's only until one of my kind get him behind closed doors and then he is on male pussy or sick pussy. A lot of men in prison do indulge in one way or another, fucking or getting sucked up. A lot of the men feel there's nothing wrong with getting some head and I agree with them, because giving a man head gives me the opportunity to turn him out. I get full pleasure out of seeing a man fall weak over me. It's only natural and inevitable for the men in prison to become excited, aroused with the desire to want to fuck one of my kind. How can they not when they are confined for months and years around nothing but men and can't be with no women physically. So when they see one of my kind looking all good and like a woman with a nice firm round ass, wide hips wearing tight jeans, hair hanging long and styled, smelling sweet and speaking with a sexy voice, of course we're going to be enticing and alluring to their sexual desires of the need to release all that built-up pressure inside of them. Some of us actually have real breasts like myself, you know. We are the best thing they're going to get, and for some, the only thing. I have also witness a lot of marriages being broken up when an inmate start indulging in the goods. I myself have destroyed plenty of marriages, not intentionally. My tricks tend to fall in love with me and want a commitment, and to prove his loyalty he ends his relationship with his wife on the streets. It even gets so bad some start denying their family visits just to keep an eye on me from fooling around with anyone else. Some of the inmates are not shy about letting it be known they are into homosexuals and you have some that would even kill another inmate over us.

"What about the drugs?"

If you are trying to ask me about us smuggling drugs or getting it inside the prison, most of my kind does both. We normally try to hook up with the main drug dealer on the yards to see if he needs a mule. If he does, then he arranges for an outside contact to get approved on our visiting list. Once the approval goes through we'll get a visit and the visitor brings the drugs to us and I keister them and take it back into the prison.

Of course, I don't do anything for free. The going rate for such a service is a quarter or a third of everything that is brought in. It all depends on the agreement between you and whomever you're working for, but most likely it would be a third without any complaints or need of negotiation. That's the going prices in majority or the prisons.

"Are all homosexuals in the prison part of the GBG?"

I am afraid not. We don't take just anyone into our society. We do pick and choose in order to keep the loyalty real and the foundation strong, but we still look out for the other homosexuals from time to time. One of our main things is to keep the GBG family dealings, activities, gatherings, missions, and attention out of the public and the institutions eyes and ears. We have been so low key for years that a lot of inmates themselves knew nothing about the GBGs, only but a chosen few who had major business dealings with us.

"Are the members of your gang one race or is it a mixture?"

We are a gang that represents homosexuals, and we don't play that racial shit like these other gangs do in these prisons and on the street. We also don't get into the prison politics. We are neutral. We have no allegiance to no one but GBG members and other Gays. We have no alliance to any groups. Our adversaries are police and anyone who feels the need to treat us unkindly. And honestly speaking, our dislike for the police is only because they have arrested most of us and those quarrels are a host within our own selves.

"What race has the most problems with gay dudes?"

Who else do you think? The damn Southern Mexicans, and that is only when a Mexican homosexual hits on one of them. They don't like for a Mexican to be gay. They say it is a disgrace to the Mexican race. And under no circumstances they are allowed to walk the yard. That shit caused a full-fledged war with GBGs, which brought the Blacks, others and Northern Mexicans to back our play against the Southern Mexicans and the whites.

For one, the GBG, being that there are different races in the Gay Boy Gangsters and when they see the Gays getting down with the Southern Mexicans, all they saw was multiple races fighting and stabbing Southern Mexicans and the other races took up the fight and it was an all-out war. There's only designated yards where Mexican homosexuals could walk without their life being in immediate danger by the Southern Mexicans.

"How do men in prison become gay?"

Well, some of them already were gay but just been in the closet. Then you have those who like to indulge in the sexual pleasures as top or just like getting some head, and they think because they are not getting fucked, that don't make them gay. The formal identity would be bisexual, but the facts stands on its own merits; they are gay but just in denial.

I cannot give you a correct answer to the question. I can only tell you of what I assume and witnessed on several different occasions. I have seen men come into the prison with feminine ways that are weak physically and get turned out. You have duties in here who looks for those types, especially for the young men who come to prison for the first time that have no sense of awareness, are easily persuaded, intimidated by fear of the unknown and vulnerable to any deceptive, illusory friendly smile and comforting shoulder. They become the victims of sexual assaults who end up submitting to the ways of life as a homosexual for the protection and that emotional shield of feeling safe. I know because I am one of those vultures who like turning out the young men who come to prison. I like the feisty ones. I'm not into the raping, but I am a master and big participant in alluring and persuading my prey to indulging into my sexual pleasures, and once they do and feel comfortable with me, then I make my move to break in that young virgin booty hole. There is no going back once I let them crawl all up in me for free. They are going to give it up or there are going to be some serious problems.

"I thought you said you were not into raping?"

I am not. I don't see that as rape. I see it as a fair trade. I give them some of my pussy in return for some of that young ass. A fair trade is not a robbery, and if I have to clip a chin to get my issue, than that's what a bitch has to do, but I am going to get mine. I call it a favor for a favor, and if they are men they shouldn't be going up in me in the first place. In prison a person has two choices, no in between. You are either a predator or a prey. And you have to remember prison is not a temporary place for me, it's my home and I have to be as comfortable as possible and every chance there's an opportunity that I can crawl up in something tight and young that comes in, I am going to. And I am not the only one who thinks like this. We have the real booty bandits running around the yards that are waiting to catch him some fresh meat to knock out and drag up into his room. Sometimes all you have to do is get them high on some Black Girl. If they never did drugs before, they are going to be super high. There wouldn't be any strong resistance then. It's just like taking candy from a baby.

"Do homosexuals have to be housed with another homosexual?"

No, classification cells every one up by their ethnicity and with a member from the same gang you are from. If you are part of a gang and they don't have any open cells to house you with one of your members, they would house you with a non-affiliate. This also could become a problem because there is no such thing as non-affiliate. Some guys come to the prison and say they are not affiliated with any gang when the truth is they are part of a gang but just don't want the administration to know about it. The problem starts when a person is assigned to a cell with a non-affiliate when in all actuality they are a gang member or affiliates or he might be one of your rivals. Plus, prison gangs have rules that none of their members are to be housed up with homosexual.

Life is no joke; it is nothing to be taken lightly. At any given moment for no reason at all someone could just wake up in bad mood and want to stab someone, and you just might be the one who he picks.

PRISON SECRETS
Eugene L. Weems

CHAPTER 9

WOODS

"What is the Wood Pile?" I asked.

We are regular Woods, white boys who believe in white pride. We are branch from our big brothers the Aryan Brotherhood, "The Brands." We call ourselves the Wood Pile because of the number of Woods we have in the family and when we come for you we are coming in a pile, in a big number. We are not racist like the Skins or the NLR; we are just for our people the superior white race. We love ourselves.

"What is the difference between the Wood Pile and other white gangs?"

We are more laid back; we not are into doing hard time and always looking for something to get into. We just want to kick back, do our dope, go to the visit and see the old lady, finger bang the cunt a little, fuck with who we choose to fuck with, score some dope, and keep a smooth program going. We are not into cutting our hair all bald. Some of us like it long. We do not follow other peoples' ways. That's why we do what we choose. We buy our dope from who has the clove at the time when we run out. We don't give a damn what color they are. Dope is dope as long; as it's good there are no complaints. The Skinheads run their little program like they are in a military school. Too many rules, wrinkled mad dog faces and seem to always have something to prove. They keep their head shaved to inform other Woods who they are. They don't buy from or deal with the African Americans. They have a straight hate for Africans and Mexicans and mainly anyone that's not white, but they especially don't like Africans and they feel all whites should. If you are not in agreement with their beliefs, you basically made an enemy, but the Skins are under us. When it comes to the Wood Pile and the Skins, we will regulate to put them back in their place. We only accept them because they are our people and also my big bros requested that we keep the peace between us. The Skins are also the Brand's extension of military to be sent on missions that need to be handled, but we have went to war and it was an ugly sight on both ends. Their numbers are large as well and still growing.

The NLR are our comrades -- well, were our comrades, I should say, until my big bros stamp them with the green light. Lately we haven't been killing each other and that's because we all needed to stick together to deal with the problems with other races to keep our numbers strong. But the NLRs seems to always be on a death wish. They just love trouble and keeping tension in the air. They used to be the Brand's side arms before they started trying to take over the California prisons. They have taken over a lot of yards in California and from time from time we do war.

The Wood Pile membership is huge and reaches out nationwide. Some programs are manned differently than others, but we are the Wood Pile.

"When a Wood comes to prison what do the Woods do?"

First he would be approached and questioned who he is, where he is from. We want to know his full name, were he lives, what gang he represent, what he is locked up for and how much time he is doing. We need to read his paperwork with the charges on it. We need to make sure he is no Chester. We don't allow rapists or Chesters to walk the yards. We kill them right on the spot. Sometimes we may even fuck them first and stick a mop handle and some other objects up his ass before slicing the cock sucker's throat. If we are tweaking off some meth, we will experiment with him. Tie him up, stick him under the bed, or tape a freak book to his back, grease him up and go to town. We let the rapist see how it feels to have some Wood up in him. There have been times when we let a rapist walk the yard because he had big money and the Woods agreed so we could get the money. We had him believing that we understood what he done was just a mistake and we are offering him a chance to clean it up by paying rent. Once we tap his money service, then we send him out in a body bag. A lot of my Wood comrades wouldn't care how much money a Chester had and what we could milk him out of; they want blood on a knife right then and there, no exception.

However, if the Wood come into the system and he is clean, then we set him up with a care package, but we do expect the things we issue him to be returned whenever he makes it to the canteen. But if a Wood comes in and he is a lame, we will take him under the wings and tax him, and if we don't, the NLR or the Skins will. We normally look for the youngsters to come into the system so we could school our soldiers to be sent on missions. We pump their small minds up with the white pride teachings with an understanding that the white race is the superior of all others. We tell them whatever they do, do it for white pride, the Wood Pile. The teaching normally gets them pumped up along with a line or two of meth straight to the brain that gets them wired up ready for action and gives them heart to tackle any task bravely.

"How does the Wood Pile make money inside the prisons?"

Just like everyone else, sell a little dope here and there and party with the rest. We have different hustles. Some do tattoo work, make wine, draw portraits and cards, fix appliances, sell food from the kitchen, tax lames, do legal work. There are a lot of different hustles we do to make ends meet. It all depends on what type of trade you have or what you like doing. Me, I like giving orders to other Woods and collecting my share of the dope that is brought in and go shoot me a nice shot of dope and tweak off of making picture frames out of potato chip bags or play Dungeons and Dragons with my cellmate, but I have a lot of comrades who hustle consistently with nothing but working fags and women out of money. They play those internet circuit web sites, placing personal ads on them for pen pals and romance. When they write they sell them a lot of dreams and a lot of them fall for the lies that's being told and send money, packages, magazines, books, basically whatever is being asked of them. The fags really pay well. I even have about seven that I write to. Most fags are easy pickings. All they want is for you to write them letters with wild sexual prison fantasies and they run with it. They love that shit and pay to keep it coming. All you need is a handful that is dishing out from $25 to $50 a month; a Wood could live comfortably inside the prison. It is all fair; you want to play, you must pay.

"Does the Wood Pile have a mandatory workout?"

It's mandatory for all Woods to work out. It is requested that every Wood put in two hours of activity every day; bar work, calisthenics or road work, it doesn't matter. It is a must we stay fit to some degree. As long as a Wood stay in shape enough to swing, a bone crunches swiftly without being winded, then that's all that matters. The size of our knives make up the difference of what we have deprived our bodies physically. Too many of us Woods like to party, It's a common fact that we enjoy using dope. As long as it is around we going to continue to use. We Woods do not have any shame in our game. We are hogs, Vikings and down for our dirt.

"How does the Wood Pile view the police?"

We all hate the god dam pigs. Fuck them all in their asses with a black dick, nark mother fuckers. It would be nice if we inmates could just all come together and kill all those bastards, but there are so many undercover rats among the inmates, we would be ratted out before the groups could put something together as massive like that. In the California prisons in the high security level fours, all the prison gangs have come to an agreement that when a pig hurts an inmate, each race has to stab a pig, and that's how it's been going down. It's prisoner's law now between the whites, Mexicans and blacks. The others, those pieces of shit aren't going to do nothing but tuck their tails and conform to prison rules. I hate those foreign sons of bitches. They always got their noses up the pig's ass. That's why we keep our foot on their necks and make them pay to stay on the yards. They pay well also and they come in handy when we Woods are on lockdown and can't make it to canteen. We just send them to the canteen to get what the Wood Pile needs. They know not to deny us or we would wreak havoc on their parade and rape their cells of anything of value when we come off lockdown. My people don't see eye to eye with the pigs. We give them mutual respect and stay out their way. We have a policy not to get friendly with no pigs unless it's one who's committing felonies for the Pile, bring in the dope sack, and even then we would stab his ass if we had to. There are only two things that we really give a shit about and that's keeping the white race strong and our dope.

"Does the Wood Pile have any other allegiance with other gangs in prison other than white?"

The Surenos who are the Southerner Mexicans, South Siders, whatever you want to call them, we have an understanding with them. It's been established many moons ago that against the blacks they catch our backs and we catch theirs. The northern Mexicans ride with the blacks, so any time we clash heads with either group we know that most likely we will have problems with both; the other race just going to wait in the cut to jump in. But that's the same way with us and the Surenos. There are only four main races that run the prisons and that are whites, Southerners, Northerners and African American.

The Surenos and the Wood do have our little problems with each other and clash heads mainly over dope. A Wood might not want to pay up or his money didn't make it on time and a Sureno might want to tax a Wood. Plus it is over a power struggle. Every race wants the top rank, the power and respect and control of the drug flow in the prisons. We whites know we are better than all other races and everyone should bow down and conform to our rules. The Southerners feel the same way about themselves. I don't know if the northerners and Blacks feel that way or not and honestly don't care how they feel. All I know is that the white race is superior in my eyes.

"Does rape take place inside the prison?"

Of course it does, there are people who get their booty hole getting took from time to time. A true Wood is not going to let no other man take his manhood. A true Wood rather die before that happens. Those that get raped are weak links from the start and deserve to have their booty hole tampered with if he is not going to stand up for himself. I hate to admit it and I'm ashamed to do so, but in the Wood Pile we do have some cold hearted Woods who are booty bandits to the bone. And I am sure every race has them. We can't disown them; they are some solid Woods who have earned their bolts righteously with honor. They might end up raping a lame who he been getting high with. It is common for a Wood to treat a lame to a good shot of dope and then want to fuck him or get a spit shine. The Wood Pile is nothing nice. We're insane to the brain, barbarians by nature and wicked by circumstance, especially when we use white sinister. It brings the demon out and you are horny as a bessy bug. Woods gets tired of pulling on himself. Some of us need that friction of those tight pale white cheeks, if you know what I mean?

"Don't Woods have wives and girlfriends and are they ever thought about before doing inhuman acts to another man?"

Yeah, a lot of us have old ladies, but most of them run off when a Wood gets locked down. Sancho takes our place. The women start slacking on their obligation and playing games. Letters slow down, money stops coming in, phone calls being refused. So who gives a shit about what a tramp thinks. They can't even hold strong for a Wood when he's down. There is a poem that the Woods send their old ladies when he's had enough of their bullshit. It goes like this.

As I sit here on my bunk
with nothing to do.
I think of the punk
that's fucking you.
He knows of me
But yet still he clowns.
So his time will come
To be shot down.
I am able to do it quickly
I know I could.
But killing him fast
is far too good.
I'll grab your sancho
by his hair.
You'll see my anger
I no longer care.
I'll beat him down
Till my heart's content.
Till his miserable life
aren't worth a cent.
I'll put my six gun
unto his head
squeeze five times
until he's dead.
There's one shot left
this is true
this one I have saved

especially for you.
So watch your back bitch
You and Sancho are through.
When I get released I am fucking him too.
I hope this hurts
And makes you cry,
Because I know you'll be a tramp
Till the day you die.
This poem ends with me in my cell.
So good bye, fuck you
And see you in hell.

Yeah, that is how it's done. It's been floating from prison to prison. I don't even know who wrote it, but whoever wrote it was feeling just like a lot us do when the old lady moves on with her life. They always end up coming back when they think you are about to go out. Who wants a bitch that can't stay strong for her man? Those are the tramps when you get out you run through and let your comrades fuck. Then you dog the shit out of her. Get her strung out on dope and do all the worse that is possible and leave her. I tell all my comrades who ladies leave them how to do her when they get out and some do just that, and a few stay with the tramp and don't follow the plan.

"What type of advice would you give those who have not been to prison?"

I would tell them to stuff a load of dope up their asses and come on to prison. No, I am just bullshitting around about that. There is only one way I can say it, and that's in a poem, but after this I must be going. I've wasted enough time with you and your book.

> In this place of concrete valley flowers and streams of pipe and rust
>
> There is no man in this manmade hell that you can count on or trust
>
> You may think sitting in that ill cell is such a bore or drag
>
> But let me tell you something, friend I'd rather be here than in a body bag
>
> For when that cell door comes to an open you enter the real world of bitter fate
>
> You make your way to the yard and smell the stench of pure hate
>
> You see it in the eyes of those who have become stagnant by the system
>
> If you don't watch your every action you will become their next victim
>
> You live and dwell in this hate long enough and you may even taste it sometime or other
>
> It may be someone you've never met or someone you take as brother
>
> So now you heard the story my friend the story of a place called prison
>
> Take heed and make the best of life my friend for you don't want to enter the belly of the beast
>
> To all my comrades and solid Woods stay strong for twenty three that represent superior Woods

PRISON SECRETS
Eugene L. Weems

CHAPTER 10

UNITED BLOOD NATION -- UBN

"Tell me who are the UBN and were they come from?" I asked.

We are Bloods, Blood gang members from different hoods from all over the world, who have union into one solid organization. That is why we call ourselves United Blood Nation. We are one humongous family who have a common interest to prosper, to be successful, to be the most powerful force on the streets and to hold important positions in the cosmopolitan arena. What people don't know is we are not into gang banging. We are far from that foolishness. It is senseless, unproductive and plain stupid to be killing over colors and property that doesn't belong to any of us, or over a meaningless exchange of words. UBN does not engage in such ignorance or

119

participate in anything that is not conducive to our aspirations.

The UBN was started in the California prison system by my homeboy who's originally from PDL. It was established to bring all the Blood sets that were in the California prison system together as one, to eliminate feuding between us and to bring the Blood love back that had been lost by small disputes that could have been easily worked out, and to stay as a solid foundation to protect all Bloods from adversaries. The UBN were only looked at as a prison gang until my homeboy who started the UBN got with the other homeboy who is doing time in a Nevada Maximum State Prison to bring all the Bloods out there in the prisons together under the UBN. He had a vision of establishing something much bigger than just a prison gang. He was serving life and had been the leader of the Playboys Blood gang out in Vegas, and had a younger relative who was incarcerated that was about to hit the streets who was also a top rank Peru Blood, who was dependable, trustworthy and loyal. The homie gave his relative the script to what he wanted done and his blessings and his relative made the United Blood Nation what they are today, a worldwide organization that's on the streets and inside the prisons. That's how we really came about.

The criminal activities that we involve ourselves in are for financial gain to support the Blood Nation. To send the homeboys and homegirls to college and trade schools to build legal businesses, to build safe houses in every state, to support the homies that's locked up financially and to pay for legal representation when one of our members need it. Our goal is to have a UBN in every professional field of employment. That's why we send some of our members to college to get those college degrees. We want to have a link and access to whatever we need. We have members who have different functions. Everyone doesn't get down and dirty with the street life. We find out what type of talent each member has and that becomes their required duty and obligation to our family. We have crews who do nothing but robberies, push dope, boosters, checks and credit card fraud, scheme on insurance companies, file fake taxes with the IRS.

And then we have our assassin crew. This crew is the elite of the UBN. They are called the Untouchables. The majority of the UBN members will never know who are the members of the Untouchable. The reason for that is to limit any possible betrayal of a UBN member who might turn law and disclose the identity of this crew who does the killing for the UBN. The less they know, the less they can speak about. The only people who would know who are an Untouchable is an Untouchable and the captain of the UBN. Everyone else is blind to their identity. The Untouchables are our silencers. They don't hang out with the homeboys, they keep low key. Their style of dress is classy, and most of them will not have tattoos with any indication that would link them to belonging to a group or gang. They socialize and intermingle with everyone to keep the ability to infiltrate. If an Untouchable comes to prison he would most likely be classified as a non-affiliate and housed with another non-affiliate or a gang member. This person who he might be housed with might be an enemy of the Bloods, but the Untouchable would never expose himself or show any hostility or aversion. He would befriend the enemy, eat, laugh and joke with the enemy, to mislead and gain the enemy's trust. The Untouchable will find out who has the keys on the yard for the Bloods and if there is any UBN there. If the key holder is not a UBN, the Untouchable will not deal with the Bloods on the yard. If the key holder is a UBN, then the Untouchable would call to the streets to do a check on this UBN member. Once he gets confirmation that the UBN key holder is a captain, then he would pull the captain to the side and introduce himself. The UBN captain would not tell the other Blood members that there is an Untouchable on the yard; he would just inform the Bloods that he has a relative on the yard and he is not a Blood but to catch his back if he gets into any trouble. The Untouchable that's on the yard would become a great informative source for the Bloods because he would be in a position to hear things that wouldn't normally be spoken around Blood members.

The Untouchables originated out of Vegas. When the homie relative got out of prison he put much footwork into building the UBN. It takes a certain type of Blood to be part of our family, not just anybody is allowed into the UBN family. Like for instance, I said we are strengthening ourselves and building for the future so all UBN members can live well. We don't have time for hard heads, loose cannons who want to gang bang and bring heat on the family. We keep those types of Bloods at a distance. We try to avoid having any dealings with them, or we will eliminate them. We don't have time to be dealing with the envy, jealousy, resentful, bitterness and ill feelings of others. We don't like in-house problems and those who don't like to follow instructions but always like to give them. That's why we try to choose our members carefully. All of the UBN members are considered leaders. It is just there are some who hold higher rank than others. UBN is not about competing with each other; it is about achieving a common goal for a better livelihood.

We have some Bloods who choose to do their own thing and that are bool with us. As long as they keep it Blood love and not try to harm or put any UBN members in harm's way, then there will be no problem. Regardless, inside the prisons if you are a Blood but not a UBN, we will still have his back. We look out for Bloods and we are not going to let no one hurt one of ours who is claiming this red madness. We also discipline our own if any of ours step out of pocket. We don't allow for no other group or race to put their hands on a Blood, especially a Nation. All Bloods might not feel like us or might not assist us, but that's bool because we UBN going to keep it real and backing and looking out even if the love is not shown back. That is how we run our program, because when it all boils down to a Blood, it is a Blood in the eyes of the enemy.

In the prisons UBN push a hard line. We have rules that must be followed and mandatory workout program. No using any drugs other than bud, and not to come to the yard drunk or you will be chastised severely. There is absolutely no indulging in homosexual activities or we will blast you out of your boots. We have no understanding when it comes to that gay shit. We only cell up with Bloods. If you are not a Damu up, when new Blood comes to the yard, we get at him to see what set he's from and a few other basic questions like his name, and were he comes from. We don't go through let me see your paperwork stuff. If you Blood is foul he should already know how we get down, or we will blast him. So Blood that is not right is not going to be walking the main line. We will find out if there is any smut on him. We do our investigation on later days.

We make sure the Bloods that come in have what they need. New clothes, shoes, television, food, hygiene and whatever else they need to get on their feet. It's mandatory that we stay looking fresh in our appearance and stay groomed and smelling good. We have a lot of young knuckleheads and wild Bloods that come through these prisons with their pants hanging down to their knees like them Crips, and we have to immediately put a stop to that. We do not wear saggy pants. We have style in our way of dressing. When a little homie come through, we school him on the rules first, what's permissible and what's not, because if he goes and does something and get caught up into some shit, this affects the whole Blood car, so we make sure they are taught right on the laws of prison, the rules of the Blood family and the ways on how he is expected to conduct himself. If he don't have his high school diploma, his ass is going to school. There's not going to be no hanging out, kicking it with the fam bam when you got school business to take care of.

We keep a tight leash on the young ones. We don't misuse our little homies like a lot of gangs do. We strengthen our weak; we educate our illiterate and help those who seem to have lost their caricature find it. We motivate the slackers because we know what we pass down to them through our love and teaching, they will pass down to another little homie someday and the bloodline would stay strong and positive. We do send little homies on missions. They have to learn by experience, because when a war kicks off with the Blood and whoever, they will have to be accounted for. We are not holding their hands. They were man enough to do whatever they done to come to prison, they are man enough to stand up as a man. We just make sure they got their proper schooling but we always got their back. When a Blood wants to become a UBN and we decide that he's worthy, he has to blast someone out his boots. If he was to become a UBN on the street he would have to dome someone.

We don't go around killing or harming innocent people. Our targets are for legitimate reasons. We have a no exception rule when it comes to kids and old folks; they are not to be harmed under any condition. In the prison it is mandatory that all UBN be up out of bed by the time breakfast is announced and there is no sleeping until the entire program is shut down. If they are caught sleeping in their cell during the day they will be disciplined. It is mandatory that all UBN keep their cells clean and neat. We also have a kitty where extra items are kept for the new arrivals who need a few things, or if one of the homies run out of something he can just get it out of the kitty. It's also recommended that all UBN stay stocked up on hygiene and to have an emergency supply of food, coffee and tobacco in their cell just in case the prison goes on long lockdowns we won't be hurting for anything.

On every yard there is a Blood that brings in the sack, and all the UBN get an issue to slang for canteen. The UBN doesn't have to sell drugs in the prison. We normally do it because the money comes in abundance, and it allows us to save the money that is on our books for emergency purposes if we ever go to Ad Seg or the SHU security housing unit. Plus, a lot of homies like blowing that weed and they're going to find a way to get it, so we might as well get the rest of the goods and send our customers to the store for us and at the same time make that money and contribute to our cause. The Woods love that heroin and speed. If you have either one of them and it's good, they will spend. We look out for the ones who spend with us. It keeps them coming back spending their money with Bloods, because they know we will deal straight up and show love. The Indians on the yards also love that heroin. The best customers are the Asians. They like that crack and majority of the Asians who are in prison normally have money or an outside source they get money from. We never have a problem collecting from an Asian because they don't want any trouble, especially from the Bloods. Here in prison, if the Asian couldn't pay, we take it to his people and let them know about it and the debt would be on them to pay. If they refuse, then we take off on all the Asians. That goes for any group or race, but like I said, their money is good.

The south side Mexicans, Surenos, claim they don't do business with blacks. That's bullshit. If we got heroin and they hear it's the bomb, they will send a Wood to come buy the dope from us or they will just pull one of the homeboys to the side and deal business on the under. A dope fiend is a dope fiend. I don't care about what type of racial shit they're going through, they're going to go get that dope to keep the monkey off their back, simple as that. We don't even trip on their politics, because we don't care nothing about them, as long as we get our money and they respect us, then there is no problem, but soon as they cross those lines we will take off on them. But one thing I can honestly say about them south side Mexicans, although they got they little racist shit going on, they are respectful regardless what they may feel inside about you. If you get into an argument with one of them, ask for a head up fade. They will not fight any black heads up, but they will try to jump you. At least with the Crips you can get a head up fade to avoid a mass riot. Most Crips will honor the challenge, and some won't.

We won't sell any crack to any African Americans, that is asking for a problem. Plus, we know a lot of blacks in prison don't have the type of money to be buying crack at the prices that it's sold for. A ten dollar street value of crack is sold for fifty bucks. Africans like that bud and that's where the money is at when it comes to selling drugs to them. It might come eight to ten dollars at a time for a cap, but it comes daily and continuously with a huge clientele.

All UBN take an oath that is pledge to the United Blood Nation. The same way you came in is the same way you can get out, but with your own life being taken. We are serious about what we believe in and do, and if someone thinks they can take us lightly, we will dome him without a second thought. If a member of the UBN ever decides he wants to show resistance and go against us, we will make an example out of his family one at a time until we could get him. We will start killing his immediate family members. Although we have no exception to the rule about harming kids and old folks, but that exception is bent when it come to anything that is a threat to the UBN. If a kid is old enough to distinguish facial features, we wouldn't let that kid live for the simple fact it could come back to hunt a member if the kid could give a description and identify the person they seen do harm to someone. No witnesses would be left that is able to talk and point fingers. This is only to protect the UBN and its members. When it comes to us and our safety and well being, there are no rules to the game other than to do whatever it takes to keep the family from harm. When you become an Untied Blood Nation, we become your immediate family and everything else is secondary. I mean everything. If someone does something harmful to a UBN, we will do everything in our power to get him. We don't care what it takes; we must get revenge. I stress that strongly.

That's just how it goes to show the loyalty and love for our extended family. There are members who don't see eye to eye or even like each other, but they know not to let their personal dislikes get in the way of the loyalty that all members are entitled to. All the UBN don't know each other because we are so big and we are all over in different states, plus we don't have any UBN hoods. We have safe houses and our family who oversees the safe house in their state will inform other UBN members in that state that there is a relative in town and someone will come and escort him around to meet the others. We don't broadcast the Nation, it's kept on the hush. We don't mark walls and buildings up with the family name. Our thing is to stay low keyed and productive. In the prison system we are not the only Blood Gang. There are a lot of them but we are by far the biggest and extend out into every state. We are the Dogg Pound and when push comes to shove we make the decisions for all the Bloods or we will take fight on those who don't want to follow in line.

Although Crips are enemies of the Bloods for no other reason than they are a different gang that represents a different color, and many years of ill feelings and intense dislike for past acts and killings we have been doing to each other, regardless of our differences, when the Africans have a problem with another race, all Africans come together and deal with it. In the prisons we ride together when it affects the African race. All African gangs have that understanding, and if a group of Africans don't assist they will be dealt with by all the other groups of Africans. In the prisons we try to keep all the Africans from fighting each other. When there is a problem we try to deal with it reasonably without violence.

The Africans also have alliances who roll with the blacks. The Northern Mexicans, Nortenos, those are our doggs. We fuck with them in a big way. A lot of them were raised up with Africans. They are totally different from the south side Mexicans. The Northerners have style. They also rep the same color as we do. Them fools stay flamed up. They kick and act just like we do. They don't wear their heads shaved bald like them sewer rat South Side Mexicans. On the streets and the prisons we ride together. The South Siders don't like that, but they can't do nothing about it, and if they try we're just going to blast a bunch of them out of their boots. The Northerners are no punks; they know how to sling them doggs from the shoulders just like Africans do and they will do some stabbing with quickness. The South Siders are already enemies on the streets, so basically we all have the same enemies. The Crips really don't care too much about the North side Mexicans because they favor Bloods more, plus their color is red, but they don't trip with them, and we are not going to accept it.

This prison life shit is brazy, but this is our reality and if a person can't overlook it, his life could come to end quickly. Doing time is not the lick; this shit will drive a person insane. It causes you to mood swing, be sad, depressed, angry, just because you are tired of being locked up and just tired of being tired. You get tired of eating the same old shit, especially soups, seeing the same old faces, hearing the same stories, doing the same thing, going through the same problems and dealing with the same issues. Everything is the same; the only difference is it's another day just like the others. People trying to stay high or drunk to escape from this place, trying to hold onto the little sanity they might still have. Being locked up makes you forget how to be human. You're always on your guard, always forming a negative opinion about a person. The vision to the outside world is lost. You begin to look at things in a different way than you would have if you were on the streets. Ugly women begin to look good to you. Women that you wouldn't have given a second glance, you begin to cherish. You become overprotective over petty things like magazines, books, tapes, a soup, T-shirts, you name it, and some inmates will try to actually kill you over a soup or magazine.

It is not good to let other inmates use your property. I am not speaking about my UBN family. We share it all because it's nothing to us, but I am speaking in general. Some inmates will let an inmate use a book or magazine, and when it's returned he will remove a page and step to the inmate who he let use the magazine and request to be paid for the magazine because a page is missing, regardless how much the inmates try to convince the other that he didn't tear any pages out. That is irrelevant. The other inmate already knows that he is just gaming to come up on a few ends. If the other inmate refuses to pay, it will be a big issue and most likely somebody will be stabbed. These are some of the games inmates play and there are a lot of them. Now if that guy doesn't have the money to pay, then the other inmate would demand something, like some ass, head, and dinner trays. It's always a hidden motive when an inmate pulls moves like this. Prison time is more than just physical it's also mental and the hardest part is doing the mental time. If you can do the mental, the rest is a piece of cake.

CHAPTER 11

SKINHEADS

"What are Skinheads?" I asked.

A collection of superlative white men standing strong for the superior white race, we are white supreme white race. We are the white supremacy, National Socialist. We are the white force of Hail Hitler, Nazis. We do not believe in democracy unless its representatives are white supremacy. We support the white race only. We believe in superiority, racist to all colors and the government. One of our goals is to recruit as many white men as possible and give them the teachings of our superior race and build a military to take over the streets and run all the prisons. Once we can accomplish this goal, e will free all whites and pack the prisons with Niggers, Kikes, Nips, and Hat dancers, who are the light skin Niggers with straight hair, and feed them one meal a day, pull out all the televisions, radios, and slave them hard.

We didn't start out in any prisons. Nazi Skinheads were organized in society. We have Nazi support groups, websites, newspapers, businesses and other sources of advocates for us Skins. We are unlike other groups whose people don't back their play and support them. In these prisons we Skins train physically. We study the teachings of our heritage, the history of the superior race. We keep our heads shaved bald and advertise our Swazi tattoos proudly to inform all other races that we are Nazi Skinheads, the superior race. We look down on everyone that is not white and even the whites that are not in conformity with our actions. We do not socialize or do business with other races. Our words are limited to mutual respect, but on the surface of our hearts we feel other races don't deserve to be respected. Why respect them when they disrespect themselves.

Prime example, the niggers. Look at the way they wear their pants down past their big asses, their hair in girly pony tails, trying to walk cat cool but looking like apes. When they speak, the words that come out of their mouth sound distorted, probably because of the those big lips they have, but whenever you can understand what they are saying it'll be something ignorant. They also disrespect themselves and their race. But one thing we Skins do respect, admire and applaud them for is the fact they are killing off their own race. I love to hear when niggers shoot each other in drive-by shootings. I love to see their baby apes walking around dirty and living in filth while their parents are strung out on crack cocaine. I love when the illiterate apes kill each other over ghetto turf that doesn't even belong to them, and when they kill each other over red and blue. They degrade and sell their women apes, give them HIV. This is what we admire about them. As long as they continue the excellent work of killing off their own, that saves us the pleasure of killing them off ourselves. We Skins just get so tired hearing them bickering about the white man keeping them down, this and that, white man is the oppressor. It is not our fault that we are the superior race and the apes are killing and oppressing themselves. The more we give them to pacify their whining, the more they want. We gave free money and housing, food stamps, television stations, books, and even a full month to do their little bullshit festivities of the history, Ramadan. What history? They don't have any history. Yes, we hate them because our ancestors hated them and it is in our genes. We are just keeping the white tradition alive.

We feel the same way about those hat dancers. The Mexicans are nothing but light skinned niggers with straight hair who run across the border to our land and have a small army of hat dancers that can't speak English and contaminate our societies with filth. The only reason we put up with them in the prison is due to the other white gangs. They asked us to try to keep the peace. The south side Mexicans and the whites have an agreement that they will assist each other to fight against the ape niggers. That agreement has been established way before my time. We Skins feel that we need no one to back our play. We can hold our own. We don't help the hat dancers when they are at war with the niggers. The other whites sometimes do, but not the Skins. Why help when we really want to see both races dead or screaming in pain for their lives. They're doing us a favor killing each other.

We have a lot of Skins coming into the prison these days and our numbers are continuing to grow. When a Skin pulls up he basically knows the protocol: To let it be known were he comes from, who was on the yard with him, his name, charge, how much time he is doing. We set him up, school him about what's been happening on the yards and who holds the keys for the Skins and introduce him to everyone. If an unknown white comes through, we try to be the first to pull him to the side for questioning, because he might be a good white to recruit as a Skin. If he is a lame, then we will tag him so the other whites would know he is our mark and we will tax him. If he doesn't have any money, we will use him as our lackey or have him to hand wash our clothes or hold on to our knives. We will find something for him to do and he will submit to our request or we will not hesitate to bash his face in.

We are most definitely into extortion. It is not that we need the money; we just like applying pressure on lames that are not making a contribution to cause of the white empowerment over all races and creeds. Believe me, if we don't pressure the lames, someone else will out the white race. We also don't care about the age of the lame, young, in the middle or old. They're going to pay or catch hell.

One thing about us Skins; we don't care about going to war. We thrive off the feeling of danger. The adrenalin rush is so fascinating, better than any high you can get from a drug. It's more mind blowing to the extreme of insane. It is pure personified evil at its best. I guess that's the mentality you take on when being in prison for a while; you must learn how to hate, and we are good at that. We used to assist the Aryan brotherhoods and Aryan warriors in doing their dirty work until we realized they were just using us. Then we started pushing our own line and going against the grain, to focus on nothing but doing Nazi Skinhead work. They tried to push the prison politics on us, but it failed and diminished away like a water vapor when they saw we would rebel every time and take flight, no matter win, lose or draw. Now if it's not about 88 we don't want any part of it. 88 are the Skins number, the double H that stands for Hail Hitler. When we see a comrade, we greet him by saying eighty-eight. The eighth letter of the alphabet is an H so we say eighty-eight to give the two H's.

All Skins must get their colors. You must stab a Jew, Nigger ape, hat dancer or a rapist. That's how you earn your Swazi, and every time you stab a Nigger one of the letters or eights are shaded in. To be a Nazi Skinhead you must be pure white, there is no half mix white mutt's going to be Skin. It's pure white always right. We feel for a white to mix races they had to be weak from the start and their son is weak because he has been bred by a weak minded white and a weak race. We are against interracial relationships. Each race should stay with their own. And we are against slavery when it consists of having niggers living on white land, cooking their meals and cleaning white folks' homes. We are against that; it's too close for comfort.

"Do the Skinhead use drugs?"

A lot of us use drugs and a lot of us don't. I myself like smoking glass. I can get a lot done off that drug. It keeps me up for three to four days at a time. When I am tweaking I create some of my best drawing and knives. The knives I make are detailed with designs, even the plastic ones. The Skins got their dope connect. We bring in our own and spread it out among us Skins. We only sell to the Woods, no other race. Mainly the dope we get in is for personal use only to take straight to the neck. We are not into trying to become rich from selling dope in the prison like a lot of those niggers are. When we get our dope we do sling enough to get a nice issue of canteen and a little money and that is about it. Selling dope in the prison is too much of a hassle. It is already too much of a hassle getting it back into the yards. We got to watch the video cameras, the police, and rats and their rat family members, because some inmates family members who be on the visits spot someone keistering dope, they go rat you out, and then the police want to put you on potty watch or go have x-rays taken to see if you got something. Normally another inmate visitor should have stopped them from running to the police. It's easy to find out who told on you because they have to do a report on you, and if there is someone who's working in the program office like an inmate who does all the typing for the police, then he will blow the cover. Also, if criminal charges are going to be filed on you and the district attorney picks up the charges, you have to get a discovery package, and the names of the person or persons would have to be disclosed inside the discovery package.

Believe it or not, there are a lot of undercover rats on the yards and they run with the gangs, ride when it is time to ride and do all the dirt that an inmate can do inside the prison, but they will still rat you out. You have all type of guys in there that does all type of weird shit. To get an inmate they don't like and want off the yard, but are afraid to stab him, they would just drop a kite on him to the police with some bogus bullshit. I even seen some go so far as to sliding a knife in an inmate's room when he was not here and dropped a kite. When the police go search his room and find the knife, they roll the inmate up and place him in Ad Seg under investigation. There are all different kinds of tricks inmates play. That's why you have to stay up on everything and don't trust anyone; you never know what goes through the minds of individuals who have ill feeling and motives. The name of this game is survival and at any given time your closest comrade could switch up on you and take your life. There is all types of reasons people do what they do. Most guys in here want to be recognized as someone important, feared, admired, and respected. The very thought of achieving that status motivates them into doing whatever it takes to get other inmates to view him as all those things. The reality of it is that none of that means anything to a man. There are thousands of hard core killers, tough guys who are respected in prison, but it won't change anything when another man feels the need to come after you. A lame who gets fed up being pushed in the corners and treated badly and then finds the heart to pick up a knife and gut you can take all those titles away from you with the blink of an eye. A knife has no friend, feeling, morals, regrets, or regards to one's status. It is going to assault you as violently as the inmate controlling its course of action. That is why we Skins try to keep a tight military and stay alert at all times, because you never know who might want to gain a reputation off you. It is easy for an inmate to get delusional.

"What does the Skinheads think about the police?"

We Skins have strict rules. No befriending the police and to only talk to them when it is absolutely necessary. We are not into the games like other groups are, sliding their way up under an officer to get them to bring things into the prison. For one, that move can be detrimental to you and your entire military. A person should never lose sight that an officer is an officer. It could just be a setup, a sting operation. We Skins do have brains. We ponder on things before doing them. We make plans to how we will attack a situation. Dealing with the police is not ever an option that we would consider pondering on. Having any dealings with them is out the question. There is a lot of things that we Skins don't agree on that other white gangs do, and we do check them and sometimes have to war with them to get our point across. That is why we are building our military forces up strong so we can do a mass sweep and claim every yard. We Skins are going to wipe out all other white gangs in the prisons. That's the plan we have mapped out. We thought about bringing a load of dope, and all the Skins fill a syringe up with heroin and pick out a white and just plunge the dope into their necks. This was the same plan that we had for the niggers and the hat dancers before we thought about using it for the whites. It hasn't become official as of yet until all Skins over the nation agree on doing it. We want to do it in a massive way. We will give the whites a chance to except.

"Do the Skins involve themselves in rapes of other inmates?"

Skins do a lot of things that Skins shouldn't do. In different prisons the key holder for the Skins might give the other Skins leeway to do what they feel needs to be done at that time. If a situation comes up that needs to be handled, the Skin that has been sent to handle the problem chooses the method he sees fit. If he chooses to apply some pleasurable anal pain before bringing great bodily harm, then that's what he chooses to do. No one will question it. Sometimes we Skins need other ways of harming those who got an issue coming. We do get bored with stabbing someone, so we think of other things to do like take a person's manhood. That is a slow death in itself. It destroys a person mentally. We like applying this punishment to the rapists, women beater,

Chester, and rats. Then we stab them up. There is nothing like watching and hearing a rapist beg and cry for us to stop giving him something that they gave to some unwilling soul. You rape the white race, we rape you. You molest the white race, we molest you. You harm the white race women, we harm you. We will rape you then take all of your belongings.

"Where are the officers when all this raping and stabbing is going on?"

We have Skins who would be our pawn to distract the floor officers and keep their attention while we rush up in a cell. We tie up and gag our victims. Other Skins will keep watch while we do our thing. You would be amazed how willing many would just bend over without being tied up once they see that bone crusher in your hand. Some officers will turn their backs while we take care of business. There are a lot of ways we successfully get our victims. A lot of the officers that work in these prisons have families and they are not quick to place their own lives in harm's way for an inmate. If that means turning their head, that's what they will do. Just because someone is an officer doesn't make them a law abiding, honest, trustworthy person. Some who wear the badges are criminals who just haven't been caught. Many officers are crooked; not all of them, but a lot of them, and that is what makes the prison even more dangerous, because you never know who is helping who and which officers favor what race or group. We Skins seem to always get leeway with white officers over other races. That is just a fact, because we represent for the white race and they see this. We also get a lot of our information from the officers about who are ratting, rapists, or when the yard is about to be searched. A lot of them provide us with this type of information; it happens all the time.

PRISON SECRETS
Eugene L. Weems

CHAPTER 12

CRIPS

"What are Crips?" I asked.

A notorious, hostile, unsympathetic, hot tempered and violent black gang who involve themselves into every street criminal activity to make money and collect merchandise. We are one of the biggest gangs in the world with several thousand different Crips subsets. We are the blue rags. Even though there are thousands of different gangs who claim Crips, we are not all together. The only thing that makes us known and looked at as one big gang in the eyes of society is that we all represent the Crips. There are a lot of gangs that are enemies of Crips. Everyone doesn't get along and does kill each other over personal dislikes. We try to keep the hostility and animosity and personal beefs on the street, and function inside prison as a Crips family.

But my gangsters are crazy; we all are. We be going through some insane wicked and dominating shit. Every hood wants to be the head. There's always some motherfuckers who want to back up from the structure and do their own thing. For some reason, we Crips rebel against any type of established authority if it's not our own gang's authority that has been laid down. We like to boss shit, like to be in the limelight, get the recognition and be feared by all other gangs and perceived as being ruthless killers. This is our mindset. It's our motivation to go all out and do anything to get fame, recognition and respect of other gangs.

We got those we call OGs (old gangsters) who have been in the game a long time and have gotten older and a little wiser. Now that they are getting old, they try to push that soft shit about how we shouldn't be doing this and doing that, but these be the same motherfuckers who taught us how to be the way that we are today. Plus, that OG title is played out. That shit means nothing to a Crip anymore, not one who's been in the game for a minute. His ass will get tired and his reputation taken by a real loc who's not trying to hear that sentimental, heart touching, sympathizing bullshit he's pushing.

In the prison the different Crip sets function with their own group, but we do have an understanding that we as Crips will come together and ride as one. All the Crip gangs have one area that all the Crips share. Crips have their workout area, showers, outside benches, and elected spokesmen. Before the spokesmen can make any decisions for the mass of Crips, they first must go around to every hood that's on the yard and talk to the head Crip for that group, like a voting process. The majority rules. I don't give a damn. There is always going to be a lot of disagreements; that is just Crips nature.

We try to keep a Crip line going without problems between us. We have so many wild ass young locs knocking down the prison gates, coming in here with a gang of time with no damn sense, gang banging. We have to snatch their ass by the collar to slow their asses down before they get a lot of shit started without knowing it, because those United Slob Nations (Bloods) is not going to accept disrespect. They will move on a young homie and down him and then take fight on all Crips, unexpectantly catching us off guard to what is going down. One thing about them slobs, they are together and will handle their business with anyone that crosses the lines of respect; I got to give them that much. And some of those are cool once you get to know them, but they're still enemies and its Crip with us to the day we die.

The problem with us Crips, if a certain Crip faction gets into it with the Bloods, it's not like all the other Crips are going to help them. Some will, some won't. I wouldn't say it is out of fear of the slobs but out of deep hatred that a certain Crip gang may have for another Crip gang, and they feel like why should we help them when they are our enemies on the street, so let them handle their own problem. But it is totally different when it

147

comes to another gang of a different race. When a fight becomes a race issue, all the other blacks would get into it.

When Crip comes through those gates he is asked what set he's from and if any of his homeboys are on the yard. He will be directed to them and it becomes their responsibility to lace him on what's cracking on the yard and how the program is ran. Every set looks out for their own members and is responsible for their actions, and if cuzz is foul, then they must deal with him or someone else will and be ready to lift them for not taking care of their garbage. I have been Crippin' a long time and I learned the hard way.

We can't be trusted. Being deceitful is part of our makeup, and we are only loyal to ourselves. We may act as though we are loyal to our gang. We will kill, rob and bang for our gang, but if push comes to shove and it's our life and another member's life on the line, then that member is on his own. We are only reliable when there is some type of personal gain in it for us. That is why those Bloods call us crabs, because we will pull another Crip down and destroy him to get ahead of the game; that is a fact. Do you really think we give a fuck about smoking another Crip when we go around smoking niggas, their mamas, bitches, kids and sometimes whole families? Hell no! When you hang around niggas who do this type of shit, you become heartless, uncaring, and unsympathetic for a human life. There is no turning around. You're going to keep doing whatever you do and try to make sure you stay on top of the game, even if that means walking over some of your own members. The game is not like it was back in the days when Crips had unity and a purpose. Now the youngsters have put a twist on the game and they are running the show how they see fit and making the rules as they go.

"So the Crips don't have any rules in the prison?"

Cuzz listen, I'm going to say it like this. Rules are different wherever you go. Some prisons all the Crips is pushing a Crip line under one set of rules and other prisons Crips cars are doing their thing. There are the standard rules about not to be disrespecting other gangs, shit like that, but other than that, Crips are pushing their own politics. Don't get me wrong, we do look out for Crips in the pen, but there is a limit to that as well.

Every Crip car has mandatory workout programs that they do, just like every race does, for that matter. Every Crip car tries to get in the dope game, bringing dope into the prisons for sale and to use. You can clock a grip up in this bitch by selling dope to the Woods, and if you fucking with that Black Girl you can make a killing off them sewer rats. Lock one of their people in and he will sell to the rest of them. We can't stand them asses, though. We are ready to kill them bean burrito eating asses every time we get a chance. On the streets of L.A. we smoke them on a regular basis. Those sewer rats think they're better than someone else, always trying to run shit and pump fear into people, but we don't give fuck about none of that weak shit. We take it to them and let it be known this Crip isn't pushing no line on no Crips or blacks for that matter. Them sewer rats always with that racial shit. That's why blacks don't like South Side Mexicans. The bitches call themselves Surenos, whatever the fuck that means. They push a hard line on their own people and in their stoops they function under one group regardless of what set they are from on the streets. Those fools try to become part of some Mexican Mafia bullshit that's really nothing but a bunch of dope fiends who stay on lockdown in the SHU. They don't walk the main line so a real gagster could show them what this Cripping is all about. We will fill their asses up with holes. If a Crip has funk with a sewer rat, they will not scrap head up; they are too much of a coward to do that, but they will come in a pack with weapons to jump on one person. They don't like us and we sure the fuck let it be known that we don't like them by killing them off. Every time I think about them sewer rates I get heated. I love it when all the blacks go to battle against them. We are laying them bitches down and they be running like hoes. They can save that weak ass shit for their own people or those Woods, because when they come fucking around with Crips they are really playing with death, because we aren't showing no mercy. We will carve that eagle and that mother Mary tattoo or whatever they be having tattooed on their bodies.

You know the Woods are different. We will step to the battle ground and do our thing. After we kick their asses and stab up a few of them, it is like everything is cool until we battle again. We still sell them dope and do business with them, regardless if most are pushing that racist shit. As long as it's not being put out there in our face, then we don't give a damn what they push. Pecker Woods are just weird and crazy.

"How does one become a Crip?"

Cuzz, that's easy. All Cuzz has to do is say he want to be a Crip and whoever he is hanging with. Crips would jump him in. It's still the same just like it always been when a person is put on the set. It goes down like that in here too. Cuzz even might not have to get knotted up to get on the set, he might just be asked to go stab someone and that would be his initiation.

"How do Crips feel about homosexuals?"

Cuzz, what you mean how we feel about homosexuals? We don't give a fuck about no homosexuals. They are just like everybody else, to be use and abused. Some of the homies do fuck with them in a real way, celling up with them motherfuckers and fucking them and getting sucked up and acting like the punks are some real bitches and shit. You see some weird shit up in here. Niggas who you never thought that would fuck with punks be dipping around corners fucking with them. Some even let them nasty ass punks put hickies on their necks and chest. I am not with that shit, that shit is gay and a lot of Crip cars let they homeboys get away with dicking down a punk. To be punks are bad luck, but I am not going to sit up here and never say the thought never crossed my mind of getting some head from one. Some of them gay motherfuckers look just like real bitches, big asses, breasts and all. Sometimes you just have to remind yourself them motherfuckers are men and have a long dick between their legs just like you. I have seen some of the little loc get turned out by punks. They call themselves being slick creeping around with the punk. The punks trick them out of the dick and get him sprung, then the punk start flip flopping with him. You got punks who are into turning out little young niggas that come to the pen thinking he is so hard and know the game and thinking he can just smack up on a punk because he acts like a bitch. That's what you can't do because a lot of them punks can fight and are ruthless just like us. Then we got those niggas in here who are asshole bandits. All they talk about is knocking out motherfuckers and running up in him, always with the sex jokes and scoping out a victim to run up in. I don't know what's going through the minds of the sick ass niggas, but whatever it is, I know it is some real fucked up shit. And then the little locs come through with their pants hanging all around their asses. Some of the homies who are known booty bandits be plotting and hoping they mess up so he could run up in them.

Cuzz, the prison is wicket; it all goes down in here. The homies raping another homies who done raped a 'lil homie. The homie sexually assaulting homies who been bringing in the dope and not kicking down and got together to rob him and do all type of other shit to him. Then you got homies who move a 'lil homie into the room with him, getting the 'lil homie high and then running up in him. Normally, niggas who do shit like that be from the same hood of their victims and other Crips can't really say much of nothing about it, because that is a hood issue, not a Crips issue. One thing about

152

those United Slob Nations, you will never hear nothing about them raping their homies or fucking punks. Them slobs will kill a nigga behind attempting to do something like that, let alone doing it. The Muslims will also, those non-pork eating motherfuckers are not to be fucked with either unless you want some serious problems. They are like them slobs, they push a strict line. We locs are the only ones who can't get our shit together. We would be the biggest gang on the street and in prison if we could just stop tripping with each other and stop wanting to run shit when we are not capable to lead, and clean up our back yards. The Muslims and the Bloods make up for the blacks in prison. There are other gangs but we are the major ones, the biggest and spread nationwide.

"How do Crips view the police, how they feel about them?"

All black gangs hate them, especially us. It is Crip with us; the police are one of our biggest enemies. Now that this three strike law is being picked up around different states, they're trying to bust us for anything to strike us out, and we kill anything that keeps us from getting away, police, kids old folks, dogs. It don't matter; all bystanders are getting peeled. If you want to stick your nose in shit that don't concern you, we are going to put some holes in you, too. The police who wants to be super cops we are letting them have the barrels of ASKs, HKs, Uzis, Tecks, Mp-5s, anything that's going to shoot a lot of bullets, because we were trying to smoke their asses. It's already been made official with street gangs that we are holding court on the street. Shoot to kill all police when being pursued. If you're going to go to prison for life, you might as well go with a bang and kill as many police as you can before they catch you. If you get away, then you done well, but if you don't, you still done good by killing one of them. This is the mentality that has been adopted on the streets. That's why we pack heavy artillery. That's why we don't pull over for the cops. That is why we blast immediately. The stricter laws they make, the more ruthless we become to avoid prison. This is also how we think inside the prisons. Why shouldn't we kill the police if thy harm one of ours? What can they do to us when most of us already have life sentences and are already in prison? Why shouldn't we kill other inmates who push us to get violent with them; if we going to stab them we might as well take their life. That's our mentality of not only the Crips but all the gangs now. We can't even be mad at how we are even being treated, because we chosen the lifestyle we wanted to live, and when you choose to be part of a gang or be involved with criminal activities, then you should know you are not always going to be a winner, and the bad do follow the good. A gangster just has to suck it up and deal with whatever that comes his way.

CHAPTER 13

SOUTHERNER MEXICANS -- SURENOS

"What are Southern Mexicans?" I asked.

We are South Siders, *Surenos*, a Mexican gang who represents the south, the big el uno el trece. Trece, thirteen, is our number, and the 13th letter of the alphabet is M, which stands for Mexican.

"What are the differences between the South Siders and the Surenos?"

Not all South Siders are Surenos. In order to become a Sureno you must first put in work. You must earn your respect to be a Sureno by putting in a lot of work for the La Raza, our governing body. South Siders are the first stage of our gang. When you are honored to become a Sureno, you gain the respect of all South Siders who are now beneath you. A Sureno's main goal then is to reach the level of respect to be made into a big homie.

Mexican Mafia are our big homies; we are under them. We are their arms and legs. We take care of all their missions and business dealings that need to be handled. Regardless what that mission or business is, if they say do it, we must do it and it will be done. The only way to be made a big homie, you first have to become a Sureno, then you must put in a lot of work for the big homies, a lot of killings, and make sure they're receiving their one-third of all drug sales from all the South Sider gangs, and keep order in the barrios. As a prospect we are sent on many missions, and once we complete all the missions successfully and earn the trust and respect of the big homies, then we would be made, giving our number, the date that we were born and made into Mexican Mafia, we are given our own area, our own prison, our own jail. We collect one-third from all Southerner gangs in that area, and run them how we see fit. Once a Mexican Mafia, no other Southerner Mexican can harm you or refuse to do what you say or he will be taken out. The only person could bring harm to you is another big homie, Mexican Mafia.

The big homies are the ones who stopped all the South Siders from doing drive-bys and killing up our people. There are many different Southern Mexican gangs, who are South Siders that used to kill each other, but the big homies stopped all that and brought the hoods together under the SUR "Soldier Under Recognition." The big homies are a collective of Mexicans who use to be South Siders. The leaders of different Southern gangs who had the love and respect of their hoods seen how we were killing up own people, gang banging, and they came together and decided to bring everyone together and take over the drug industry and build up our barrios. Open up our own businesses, take over the hoods in each state. Any South Sider who refused to follow their orders got the green light and were killed if they don't want to follow orders. Every Southern Mexican hood are taxed one-third every month of all the drugs they sell. This money goes to the big homies to create businesses, buy land, build the hood and support those in prisons. Refusal to pay will get you the green light. All South Siders and Surenos are obligated to the big homies. You must be willing to place your life on the line for them at any given time with pride. Each and every Mexican member must be willing to sacrifice his life when honor comes available to you, and if he wishes not to do his duty, he will be taken out.

"Can you tell me how the Southerners run their program in prison?"

Every yard has a key holder who is a Sureno. He is the head for all the Southern Mexicans. When any South Sider comes to the prison we all are under one set of rules as Raza; no individual sets. All must show us their paperwork. We need to know your full name, age, what hood you're from, your nickname, how much time you got, what other prisons you've been to, and what type of tattoos you have. All this information is written down and saved. We will check to see if he is in good standing with the homies. As long as that name isn't on the green light list we get every month (people to be taken out), and he checks out okay otherwise, then we will provide him with everything he needs to make his time as comfortable as possible. He will be introduced to all the homies on the yard. His roommate is obligated to school him on how things are ran on the yard, and if he doesn't check out in good standing, we will lift him off the yard immediately.

We don't allow no Mexican rats, molesters, rapists, drive-by shooters, or homosexuals to walk the main line. We will roll them up off the yard. We try to send this type of disgrace to our race out in a body bag. There will be no South Side Mexican on the yard that is not functioning with the La Raza. We accept no excuses. There will be no "I've found God and am giving my life to being Christian," or any other religion. If you haven't found SUR, then we are rolling you up, no exceptions. Any Mexican who shows a sign of weakness, we will lift him. Weakness is not allowed among the SUR Familia.

We have mandatory rules that all Mexicans must follow. Every member must be up out of bed before the program starts. There is no sleeping while programs are up and running. You can go to sleep after the program shuts down. Your mattress must be rolled up. The cell must be kelp clean and neat. No fighting with your cellie. If there is a problem, let another member know so we can get one of them moved into another cell with a homie they can get along with. Everyone must continue their education to keep the mind strong. Your clothes must be neat and heads shaved. The reason we keep our heads shaved is if one of us stabs someone and the officer happens to see it, we can blend in with the group of the homies and it would be hard to pick out the one whom they saw doing the stabbing. All the homies have to come out to the yard when they are allowed. If not, then they get punished with 113 count burpies. If you're sick and can't make it out to the yard for whatever reason, you still will get punished with 113 count. You can either do them on the yard the next day or in the unit, but they must be done and a homie must be there to witness you doing them.

There is absolutely no prison robberies. No disrespecting the police, because if a police disrespects you, then you are obligated to stab him. So to avoid any problems is to show respect at all times. Speak to them when spoken to or when you need something that only they can issue. And never start playing with them.

Also, there are no one-on-one fights with any blacks. If one fights, we all fight. No coming out to the yard intoxicated. We have a daily workout program. It doesn't matter what you do as long as you work out for an hour and half. We are told that we are not allowed to use drugs because we must stay alert at all times, but if the key holder uses, he allows everyone else to use if they choose. On other yards the key holder may not use so we will not be able to.

"Do the Southerners rape other inmates?"

Only if they're looking to be sent out of here in a body bag. We will not accept any of our people raping

159

anyone and we will not allow for anyone else to rape any of ours. If a homie is even caught sex playing he might get rolled up, but for sure he will have issue coming and have to do lean up. When a homie has to do clean up, that is when the key holder decides that it's time to clean up our back yard. That means to lift those who are not in good standing with the Familia anymore. So those who got cleanup are the ones who have to go and lift those who need to be lifted. Cleaning house, cleaning the back yard, it means the same. If you got cleanup, duties it must be done when you are told do it. This type of duty can put a homie in bad position to getting more time if not life, because he may have to attack his victim right in front of the police, and even if the police try to interfere, it's a must that he gets his target.

"Do the Southerners sell drugs in the prison?"

Si...Yes, we push pounds of drugs through the prisons monthly, crystal meth, heroin, and weed. We sell to everyone except the Nortenos, Blacks and homosexuals. The reason why we don't sell to Blacks is because we are not allowed to do business with them. The Blacks never can deal straight. Plus the big homies had put the green light on all blacks because many years ago a Crip spit on one of the big homies in court, and ever since then we've been killing each other, especially in Los Angeles, on the streets, in the jails and in prison. We have been going at it for years. Plus those Crips feel they are running things and always disrespecting us. We Surenos have a real big hate for Crips.

We sell all our drugs to the Woods and the others. We never have problems with the others, but the Woods tend to be slow about paying. If someone would get a nice size Clavo from us and can't pay, we'll slap the debt on his people. If they refuse to pay, then we go to war. That's why we now have a policy not to give Wood more than a hundred dollars worth of dope at a time. Once they pay, then we will sell them more. We make big feddy off of drugs. Drugs is how we support our gang in prison. This is how we keep our girls coming to visit and bringing up the clavos. We buy transportation for certain girls so they could carpool and bring the other girls up to visit the homeboys. Any dope that the homies bring in, we must give a third of it to the key holder. Basically, we are paying tax, and if we have a problem with collecting money from someone we sold drugs to, we just let the key holder know and he will send someone to do the collecting.

"Why is the green light on all Blacks and not just the Crips?"

The reason is due to when a Mexican kills or harms a Crip member, the Bloods jump in because they look at it as a race issue, then we have to war with them over something they don't have nothing to do with. The big homies know it would happen like this because the Bloods always end up backing the Crips or the Crips end up backing the Bloods when it come fighting any race other than black. That's why he put the light on all blacks. We really didn't have problems with the Bloods. We used to do a lot of business on the streets with the

UBN, but that ended when they decided to get involved in our business and killed a few homies and robbed them for a bunch of heroin and crystal.

"What's your relationship with the Nortenos?"

Nortenos are our arch enemies. They want the same thing we want, to control the streets, drugs, prisons and have the power. We got a big hate for them because all side black Mexicans are always trying to act black. They talk like blacks, dress like blacks, walk like blacks, hang with blacks, listen to black music, eat and drink after blacks. That why we call them blackxicans (Black Mexicans). They even ride with blacks on the streets and in prison. They normally hang strong with the Bloods because both gang colors are red. They need to learn how to stick with their own race.

"How do you feel about the Woods?"

We don't care for any of them like they don't care for us. We been riding with each other for a long time, but we don't need their help. Woods think they are the superior race, but we know that we are the SUR, and we sometimes have issues over this. The little Nazi Woods are a true hate group and we know they don't care for us at all, but we will take flight on them all. It has happened before on many occasions. All we request from all races is respect. Give us respect, we will not have problems. Disrespect us, we will go to war.

CHAPTER 14

NORTHERNER MEXICANS -- NORTENOS

"What are Northerner Mexicans?" I asked.

Chicanos from the north side. We are the Northern Familia, Nortenos 14. The Northern family is a gang of North Side Chicanos who come together to protect our hoods, to build and support our communities, to establish our own businesses, markets, make a better life for our families so we can get out of the ghettos and own our own homes and send our folks to colleges. We gangsters choose to put our lives on the line every day to make our vision a reality. We place ourselves in dangerous situations of being killed or sent to the pen for life in order to make money to build our dreams. Most of us are into criminal activities, pushing the dope, robbery, jacking drug houses, jacking cars for chop shops. You name it, we do it. It's all for the cause for the establishment and strengthening of the Northern Familia enterprise and communities. We are paving the way for our ill brothers, sisters and cousins to be able to have opportunities that weren't available to us. We have done well so far with or vision and goals. We got many business of our own and provide jobs to the homies, car clubs who support fundraisers, record labels, markets, car washes, and many of our folks are going back to school and colleges even some of the homies is stepping into the trade schools.

"Why so many of you going to prison?"

Like I said before and I'll tell you again, we involve ourselves in criminal activities to make that money or have to put an enemy to rest who threatens the Familia. A lot of us are so caught up into the gangster lifestyle that we refuse to change our ways. We'd rather be involved in doing the dirty work and allowing the younger generation to live out our dreams for us. I know that sounds crazy, but it's real. Some of us can't read or write and have been in the street life all our lives and involved in so much shit trying to make ends meet, for us to go back to school would be a waste of our time. Our minds have already been programmed for one thing, to survive by the streets. So gangstas like us are pushing the young homies into staying in school to be better than us, not just like us. When you're doing dirt, you're bound to get caught up, and we all know the punishment for that, jail, prison, or the graveyard. When you are in the lifestyle of being a gangsta, you don't think about those consequences.

"How do you run your program inside the prison?"

We run a smooth program with strict rules, but still a smooth program. A new homie that comes through, we holler at him to get a feel for who he is and where he is from. We run down the rules, find out if he needs anything, and if so, all the homies would pitch in a nice care package, and if one of the homies who has an extra radio, they would shoot it his way to use.

We keep the family clean of the molesters and rappers. The homies do everything together. We all keep a close eye on each other. Our numbers aren't always big in prison and those sewer rats like to trip when they see us outnumbered. That's just how they are. They won't box because they know me have major scraps. The only thing they would try to do is rat pack you three on one, so we have to stay ready and keep big knives just in case they run up.

We hang out with the Blacks. We use the same phones, showers, workout area, eat at the same tables with them. We feel more comfortable around Blacks. Most of us grew up with Blacks and have black friends, so it's a love thing. The sewer rats feel that we try to be like the Blacks. They say we are a disgrace to the Mexican race. They call us Blackxicans. We don't trip; we just handle our business every time they feel like they want a problem. When the homies are short in numbers, the Damus always catch our back. We are a lot closer to the Damus than any other Black gangs. They always have been straight with us from the beginning. Those Crips are the ones we're leery of. Just put it this way. They can't be trusted and that's real, too scandalous. We try to keep all dealings with them at a minimum. They really don't like us that much because we kick it with the Damus, though. The United Blood Nation, Blood line, and Pirus (original formation of the Blood gang), they are some real cool people, and if a Damu tells you something, you can basically depend on it. Most of them are loyal to their word and are not disrespectful.

The Woods, we only put up with them because that's one of the biggest money sources for the drugs. We make a lot of money off the mint leaf, trees with the Blacks, but the heroin and crank, that's the Woods drugs and they would give up everything in their cell for a fat paper. The other's money is also good, but they don't buy as much as the Woods do. Plus, when the sewer rats are not in pocket they use the others to come and buy the drugs from us. We bring in our own dope or work with a Damu to help us get it in if they got the hookup. We usually help each other. The money that we make from selling drugs in the prison, we break bread with our ladies for personal use, to recoup, and expenses. To put money to live inside the prison, especially if you want a homo stabbed. There are other races who do fuck around with punks, but that's their business. Our business is Northern Familia, fourteen's business.

"How do Northerners feel about the police?"

We don't like any police because we are on two different sides. We do blast on the police on the streets and in prison. We are not into making friends with them, but we'll do try to get friendly with a female officer so she will bring in the drugs. Even some male officers are just as easy to get friendly with, especially the rookies. Everyone likes money and don't mind making a little extra. We have been having our homeboys and homegirls who haven't been in any trouble apply for correctional jobs so we could have some inside assistance to look out for us.

"Do the Northerners use drugs?"

Yeah, some of us. Some of us like that tree, some like the other stuff. We do our thing. We even make wine and the homies will kick it, drink and smoke. Like I said, we run a smooth program. We just demand that our comrades follow the mandatory rules of the Familia and stay in shape and ready for war at all times, and to never lose sight to where they are. Everything else is all good.

We never have to worry about materials for knives. As long as we got plastic mop buckets, we can make knives. There is a lot to deal with in the pen, too many crazy people with no sense, too much time on our hands with nothing to do, too much stress. The only way of releasing it is with violence sense that's the easiest and first thought that comes to mind. You can always find someone who is willing to challenge you. Fist fighting is out, but knife playing is in. This is the prison way for all races. Every race, gang, and individual in prison is dangerous, because you never know how a person is thinking from one day to the next. No one in the pen can be taken lightly regardless how big your crew is, how tough and feared you are, no matter how many stabbings or killing you've done. None of that means anything to a man who is out to get you.

You must play it smart and overlook some things and keep your emotions in check if you want to make it in the pen. Most everyone in here has this mask on, hiding their true self, and when a person keeps that mask long enough, he becomes that very mask. Honestly speaking, many times at night when I lay in my bunk thinking, I wish that I had never ever gotten involved in the criminal lifestyle. I wish I had gone to school and didn't hang out with the homies smoking and drinking and doing crime and everything else we did. If it wasn't for me wanting to be cool and hang out and get the reputation that I have now, which don't mean nothing to no one but me and my homies, I wouldn't be locked up with all this time I have to do. I wouldn't be going through mental trips with myself at night. I wouldn't be in so much emotional pain, having to watch my back every day all day. I wouldn't have to eat soups and chips and peanut butter sandwiches when I get hungry or smell another man's shit or listen to him piss every day. I wouldn't have to worry about my girl out there giving up the panties to somebody else and hoping she'll write to me. I wouldn't have to wash my clothes out of buckets, the sink, or the toilet. I wouldn't have to worry about if today is going to be my last day on this earth. I wouldn't even be thinking about all the people in my family I hadn't told I love them. If only I wasn't a dumb ass who chose this bullshit lifestyle, I would be at home right now thinking of none of this, living life on the streets. Even if I was poor and had nothing, no friends, no money, no girl, no home, no family, and no identity, I would accept that and be grateful rather than be locked up. If there was a way that I could give my old life back just for my freedom, I would give it all back, the keys to the gang, my rep, my name, my homies, the money, Low Riders, everything. I hate to say it, but even my race I would give back to live that square life. But since that's not possible, I might as well keep being that gangsta that I am to the fullest, and keep my personal thoughts to myself. I am sure everyone on this prison has wished one time or another that they would have made a different choice. They may never admit it, but the prison itself is the toughest, hardest and coldest gangsta that is, who can never be killed. That's the real key holder.

PRISON SECRETS
Eugene L. Weems

CHAPTER 15

LYLE MENENDEZ

Who is Lyle Menendez behind the prison walls? Is he that notorious killer that the media portray him to be? Do the inmates look up to him and/or respect him? Is he treated like a celebrity? What does he do on a daily basis? What does he eat, wear, and who does he hang out with? These are some of the questions that I'm normally asked by associates who learn that Lyle and I are friends. I came to the conclusion that people are just curious by nature and infatuated by the psychotic acts that all people are capable of committing.

I know many of you reading this may be wondering how could I or why would I want to befriend a man who's a murderer like Lyle Menendez, a man who is labeled a notorious killer. The truth is, his criminal activities, behavior, reputation and title does not affect me, because my entire life I somehow engaged socially, lived among, conducted business with and befriended people with criminal diversity disorder such as his. Anyone is capable of embracing and/or engaging in violent acts, and knows that life behind prison walls has its vengeance no matter race, culture, sexual orientation, wealth or crime. The past is never dead and buried. I myself am no saint, my criminal history is far from innocence. I suspect that I've become accustomed to the ills that consume peoples' souls, hearts, and lives by growing up around people involved in some type of criminal activity. So befriending Lyle was nothing out of the ordinary. We are more like business associates than friends. I'm more of the retailer and he's the customer.

Before I personally met Lyle I had heard people talk about him as if he was some type of celebrity. I was well aware who he was and why he was in prison, but I was not impressed by the senseless crime he was convicted of that made him famous. Personally, I sure did not view him as a celebrity, but yet I sit here and compose these words about him and our dealings. My perception of him is of a damn fool who came from a privileged family and who had a promising future. A man who allowed his desires for wealth to overshadow his better judgment, magnifying the temptation to murder his parents.

What I've come to learn about Lyle is that he's very educated. He has the tendency to look down on those who are underprivileged. He's very arrogant and feels he can outsmart, outthink, manipulate and control people. But one thing for sure, his college education didn't prepare him for the life he's living and the people he would encounter behind the prison walls. What he was so illiterate to was that the prisons confine some of the most criminal minded geniuses in the world who are considered to be professional manipulators, serial killers, robbers, gangsters, and a host of titles of intellectual criminals.

I had been introduced to Lyle through a mutual friend by the name of Terry *T.P.* Prince. We had been housed at Mule Creek State Prison, a California correctional facility where they housed the high notoriety inmates, celebrities, ex-judges, lawyers, district attorneys, gang lords, serial killers and the most looked-down-upon pieces of shit, rapists and child molesters.

T.P. is a golden brown complexioned African American inmate who is well built for being in his fifties, with a fast and pearly white grin. He has a handsome face and brown eyes that smile silently among his peers. He's a guy who is respected at the utmost level by the prison population and staff. Very intellectual, business minded, productive, influential, and always willing to help those who seek to change their negative behaviors. And he is very dangerous with a pen and paper.

Lyle had targeted in on his savior and befriended T.P., knowing if he became good friends with T.P., that alone would protect him from many of the dangers that lurk the silent shadows of the weak. Lyle may have been a murderer and known to the world as a cold-blooded killer, but behind these prison walls he was considered a coward and a rich gay boy among the prison population. His status was one level above child molester. Believe it or not, criminals do have a code of conduct to what type of criminal acts are acceptable and those that are looked down upon, and there is always predators drifting the yards for prey to victimize. From my standpoint, understanding the criminal way of thinking, Lyle was a prime golden goose waiting to be plucked.

His daily activities during the weekdays consist of phoning his wife after 8:00 a.m. and going to the prison yard either to go to the inmate canteen, work out, play soccer, play chess or perform his MAC duties. MAC is an acronym for Mens' Advisory Council. Lyle is the vice-chairman and T.P. is the chairman. They represent the prison population and deal with the prison wardens, captains, sergeants, and other officials. You would think that the general population would have boycotted the election of Lyle as vice chairman, but just like any other democracy, there is always some type of scheme and deception going on in the background. Let's just say if it wasn't for Terry, Lyle would not be on the MAC.

Lyle took a liking to me for several reasons. One, my reputation among inmates, and secondly, my philanthropic and entrepreneurial spirit. He knew that I was a professional kick boxer and author, and that I had been working on several book projects, one about heroes titled *United We Stand*, and secondly, a book that would help at-risk youth. I had asked him to write the forward for the youth book. We talked at length about my vision and why he would be a positive contributor. Lyle then suggested that I also speak to his lover, a slip of the tongue on his part. He noticed the confused expression that appeared on my face and before I could inquire about what he meant about speaking to his lover, he corrected himself. "You might want to talk to my cellie; he may be interested in sharing his story. He is an ex-gang member named Chino. He is at work now in PIA (Prison Industry Authority). If he agrees to help you with the project, then I will do the forward, but I can't do nothing concerning my case. I would like to read some of your work when you get a chance."

My mind was deadlocked on his suggestion that I speak to his lover before he switched up and corrected his statement and said his cellie Chino. Is Lyle gay? I asked myself, while staring in his hairless face trying to locate a hint of femininity about his appearance or demeanor. I forced myself to shake the thought.

Later that day Lyle introduced me to his cellie Chino, a handsome Hispanic man who had a body-builder's physique and sported a thick goatee and tapered haircut. I eyeballed his demeanor searching for any hint of an unconventional sexuality. I don't know why I was so curious because I was not homophobic and really didn't care the least about his sexual preference. I think I was just taken by surprise to what Lyle had said earlier and knowing what he was in prison for, and how his look didn't fit the image and demeanor of a gay guy. I was curious and my need to know subconscious attitude kept me probing silently for answers just to ease my mind.

I briefed Chino about the youth book I was in the infancy stage of composing and how he could assist me in my plight. I informed him of what Lyle stated concerning his willingness to participate. Chino agreed to help and soon after Lyle concurred.

Months had drifted by and my full attention had been redirected to another book project that was more important to me, *United We Stand*, a tribute to the American Soldiers and the fallen heroes of the war on terror. A book I composed to support our troops and families, and to show my love, respect, and appreciation for them.

I wanted to implement a fundraiser at the prison for the sole purpose to raise money to buy copies of *United We Stand* from Mule Creek State Prison inmates to be sent to our troops overseas. My personal attempts got me nowhere other than a CDC 115 Rules Violation Report, which I was charged and found guilty of business dealing for sending flyers to my outside correspondents (family and friends). (See Exhibit B at the end of the book.) Prior to receiving the CDC 115 rules violation report, I had approached Lyle and T.P. for their assistance, being that they were on the Mens' Advisory council and had a good relationship with the prison administration. They agreed to help because they liked the idea. T.P. submitted the proposal for donations to purchase books for American troops. (See Exhibit C at the end of the book.)

In the course of attempting to get the approval for the fundraiser project, Lyle had been reading several of my short stories and unpublished novels. He liked them so much he frequently asked to read my writings. I started to become suspicious to why he wants to keep reading more of my literary creations. I asked myself was he trying to steal my writings or was he just infatuated with the urban street tales I write about? It's common for a prisoner to think the worst about another prisoner, and I was no exception to the virus of thinking the worst about people behind the walls.

Several weeks later Lyle inquired about how long it would take me to write a book. He goes on to say he has been thinking about writing one of his own, and that he has a well known journalist ghost writing his autobiography. As an entrepreneur and opportunist, I asked him which one of my unpublished novels he liked the best. He liked several of them, but leaned toward his favorite. I then proposed a question "How would you like to co-author that novel with me?" I let you put your picture on the front cover, and your name as co-author?

Before he could answer T.P. spoke "Don't forget me. I want in on it." At first I thought T.P. was joking, but when I turned to face him I seen that he was dead serious. I had no problem with allowing my boy to get a piece of the pie.

Lyle thought that would be a good idea. He said he would be willing to co-author the book with me, and requested that I draft up a contract. Lyle, T.P. and myself stood on the prison yard discussing the intricacies to what should be added in the contract and what percentages would be appropriate, now that T.P. was in the equation. I made it clear to Lyle that I will be keeping full control of my literary and movie rights. He had no problem with that. Being that I was the A-yard visiting room photographer, Lyle suggested that he take a few recent photos for the book, and I agreed. That following weekend during visitation with his wife he took several photos for the book. I had been prepping the manuscript for publication and making plans to have the book cover prepared. He didn't like the photos and informed me he will take more at a later date, which he did and gave them to me, many months later.

Lyle is the type of guy who likes to do things when he's ready. He has the demeanor that he's better than everyone else, and is very manipulative. Most of the correctional officers treat him as if he's more special than other inmates. They allow him to do things and have things that others wouldn't be allowed to have. Here is a guy who has a pet lizard. Now, what prison have you heard of that allow inmates to have reptiles as pets in their cells? Well, Lyle Menendez has a pet lizard. Every day when the yard is open you can find Lyle on the yard searching for bugs, crickets, frogs and trying to catch flies, bees, and dragonflies with a plastic bag so he could feed his lizard.

I had the pleasure of meeting his wife. Working in the visiting room I got to see her every week. She's a beautiful and sexy woman, very classy with a threatening edge of excitement. Always cheerful and showcasing her gorgeous smile. She loves cats. Lyle would always ask me if I could bring out his cat magazines to the visiting room so him and his wife could enjoy them together. Inmates weren't allowed to bring out magazines to visiting, but being that I worked in the visiting room, I was able to. Lyle and his wife would normally request a table on the outside patio where they would sit and flip through the pages of magazines. Sometimes they would play board games while sharing snacks. Lyle and his wife show a lot of affection, more than what any other inmates were allowed to demonstrate.

Since I've known him, not once had I seen him eat in the dining hall. He chooses not to eat any of the food that is served to the prison population. He prepares his own meals in his cell. He cooks his food in a 350 watt hot pot and on a makeshift hot plate. He recently stopped eating meat and became vegetarian. He is allowed to purchase food from inmate canteen, a maximum of 220 ounce a month (see exhibit D). Please note the canteen ordering from is the items that inmates at Mule Creek State Prison are allowed to order. Other prison canteen lists may be different. Lyle is restricted to the same allowable items as other inmates, one special purchase package and one quarterly package. A special purchase package consists of one of the following allowable items: one 13-inch LCD Flat screen TV, one CD player, one guitar or harmonica, one typewriter. Quarterly packages consist of 30 pounds of food and/or clothing items from approved vendors, such as Packages R Us, Union Supply Direct, Access Securepak, Inmate store, music by mail, and Walkenhorsts.

He does overshadow his peers because of his wealth. As we all know, money may not have any power, but it does have great value because it empowers one to get what he otherwise could not. He tries to be discreet, but that's virtually impossible because of his belief in the need to have the best of everything, and in excessive amounts.

Allow me to propose a question to you. When have you heard of a tennis court in a state prison for prisoners? Well, Lyle was able to get the approval from the warden to pay to have a tennis court built on a yard at Mule Creek State Prison. The tennis court hasn't been built as of yet, but it has been approved. Now that's what the power of money can do for you.

T.P. and I had been sitting on one of the prison yard cement benches enjoying the warm summer rays that accompanied a beautiful day and talking about his daughters, when we notice Lyle being tongue lashed by a short fat southern Mexican who could barely stand up straight. It was obvious that the Mexican had been drinking pruno (prison made wine). He was on tilt and looking for trouble and decided Lyle would be his victim. T.P. and I joined the spectators to watch the action. I just knew Lyle was about to put hands all over this guy in a violent way for his disrespect. Lyle had the advantage. The guy was intoxicated and threatening his life for the cowardly act of killing his parents. In my mind, I told myself that this guy's motives were more than his disapproval of Lyle's criminal acts. Somewhere in the picture he seen a financial gain, and felt like Lyle was his avenue to a payday.

The Mexican eased within reaching distance of Lyle and in a blink of an eye he had a death grip around Lyle's gold necklace and the wedding band that was hanging from it. Lyle flinched to save his neck from a fat hand that was violating his comfort zone. Before Lyle realized it, his necklace and wedding band had been snatched from his neck. He quickly felt around the empty space of his neck as if he was unsure that he had been robbed. He then took an aggressive step toward his confronter as if he was going to take his belongings back, but was immediately stopped in his tracks by the overhand haymaker that was coming his way, immediately followed by another, both hitting nothing but air. Lyle leaped out the way of the fists that meant to do him harm. I was in complete shock at what my eyes were to witness next. Lyle turned on his heels and was in a full sprint across the prison yard. He didn't stop until he was sure he was out of danger.

"Are you serious?!" I expressed to no one but myself. I was in awe, complete disbelief to what I was witnessing. So many things shot through my mind. I just couldn't believe that this cold-blooded killer was running from a fist fight with a drunk Mexican who could barely stand up straight. This guy just robbed him of his gold chain and wedding band. I was sure he would stand up as a man and fight for his wedding band at least. That ring was a momentous part of his commitment to his wife. Violation of something like that was worth fighting for. I found myself becoming upset, knowing in my heart that I would never allow that to happen to me without fighting for my belongings, win, lose or draw. That's just me. I was raised to stand up for what I believe in.

Lyle noticed T.P. and I sitting on the bench. He made his way over to us, breathing heavily. I saw fear in his eyes and noticed he was trembling. "Lyle, what up? Go knock that fool out!" I said harshly, letting him know I didn't respect his cowardly ways. My words seemed to fall on deaf ears.

"Malik, can you go try to get my chain and wedding band back?" Lyle asked, staring in the direction of the guy who tried to assault him but managed to rob him. I was now steaming hot as fish grease angry. I wanted to grab Lyle by the throat and choke the shit out of him. Here this fool was asking me to help him, to do what he needed to be doing himself. I didn't want to get involved in his problems because I know there was an extremely high possibility that if I did, it could create tension and/or most likely a race riot between the Black and southern Mexicans. But I also knew Lyle and my friend T.P. where good friends, and knew that T.P. would back Lyle to get his property back, so regardless, I knew I would have to involve myself sooner or later.

Lyle was still trembling like a mini bike. It was clear in his eyes he was scared and humiliation was plastered all over his face. "Man, I'm to help you get your shit back?" I growled. "But!" Lyle nodded his head before I could finish the sentence, understanding that he would be owing me a big favor in the future for wanting me to get involved in his troubles. It is common since among inmates nothing in prison is free.

I rose to my feet with an aggressive demeanor and started making my way toward Lyle's attacker. "Say Ese, let me holla at cha," I said to the drunk Mexican. "I am going to need that shit back you just took." I seen the inmate re adjust his attention to me, more curious if I was talking to him or someone else. I quickly assured him he was the person I was addressing. "Yeah you, I'm taken to you homeboy! I'm gonna need all that back!"

"You go need what back?" he asked after finding his voice.

"That shit you just took from Lyle," I snapped back.

"What you got to do with this, homie? You don't have nothing to do with what dude and me got going on. You protecting this piece of shit. Punk bitch, killed his parents. He can't stand up for himself. What, are you his protector or something?"

The Mexican had a valid point, and I knew I was wrong for involving myself into something that didn't concern me, but it was too late for that now. I had already overstepped my boundary, so I held my ground and position. "Fuck all that you stressing. Cough that fool shit up before it be a problem!"

"I don't have anything of his." The Mexican said, opening his hands and then raising his arms in the air so I could see he didn't have any of Lyle's property. I wasn't with the games. My mind was already made up to get on this fool's ass if he chose not to relinquish Lyle's property. I guess the Mexican seen it in my face that I wasn't playing when I started toward him. He reached into his back pocket, which caused me to pump the brakes on my attempt to assault him. I wasn't sure what he was reaching for. It could have been a knife, for all I knew. It wasn't uncommon for a inmate to be carrying a piece, and I wasn't no fool, so I waited to see what the reaching hand was about to brandish from the pocket. When the hand reappeared it was gripping Lyle's property. He slung it to the ground in the dirt. I retrieved it and returned the items to Lyle. The Mexican stumbled off toward a group of other Mexicans. I later learned the Mexican's name is Santillan inmate #F-03786.

A few days later Lyle's cellie Chino approached me. He thanked me for getting Lyle's property back. He told me that him and Lyle had something for me to show their appreciation, and when I get a chance to stop by their cell. So I did just that the following day. The tower officer allowed me access into the building because I told him I needed to speak to Lyle Menendez the MAC rep. I didn't see Lyle nowhere In the dayroom, so I asked the building clerk what cell Lyle lived in. He pointed toward the upper tier at his cell. I made my way up the flight of stairs. When I approached the cell door I looked into the cell window, and to my surprise saw Lyle and Chino laid up in the same bunk cuddling. *Ain't this a bitch!* I thought to myself. I moved from in front of the window to the back of the door and knocked. "Lyle, what's up man. This is Malik. Chino told me to stop by," I said. By this time Lyle and Chino both were at the door, both attempting to talk at the same time. I could hear it in their voices that they had been caught off guard. They were aware that I seen them hugged up in the same bed.

They slid open the cell door, Chino greeted me and stepped out the cell and strolled off. I can only assume that he was embarrassed. I waited at the cell door admiring how nice their cell was. It was immaculate and decorated nicely. I watched Lyle slide open one of the homemade painted cardboard cupboards and remove a bottle of what looked like vitamins and tossed them to me. They weren't vitamins at all. It was a new bottle of Creatin. It was something I'd been trying to get him to sell me for the longest, being that him and T.P. were the only inmates on the yard who had such supplement. Lyle had a huge quantity of it. "That's for you" he said and reached up under his bed and pulled out a clear large garbage bag of honey buns and handed them to me "I appreciate you getting my property back, Thanks." He said.

I couldn't help it, I had to know, and I wanted to hear it from his mouth, regardless of what I seen with my own eyes. So I just straight up and asked "Lyle what's up with you Chino? I seen ya'll hugged up. Are you gay?"

The answer that he gave me was somewhat shocking. "Chino is my man" Lyle said bluntly. There it was. The truth right out the Vagina mouth. There was no need to strain my mind about if he was or if he wasn't. I had my answer. Lyle asked me not to mention it to anyone else, but I already had planned to go tell T.P. what I saw and that Lyle was gay, and the bitch in the relationship. I was fidgety anticipating to tell my boy the news. I quickly said my thanks and headed for the door.

I found T.P. working out at the pull-up bars. I wasted no time telling him about Lyle. He listened to what I had to say, and once I was finished, he told me that he'd known about Lyle. "Well, hell! Why I wasn't briefed on this so I'd know this information that you've been knowing? " I said harshly.

"Man! Lyle been gay, everyone knows about him" T.P. said.

AUTHOR'S NOTES

My analysis about the prison, the different prison gangs and their functions comes from actually living within the walls. Most of the inmates don't care too much about education. As long as the drugs, cigarettes, televisions and other entertainment are available, they are content. The majority of the inmates have life sentences and have accepted the prison lifestyle and won't allow their minds to venture beyond these walls. There are a handful that stay diligently working at regaining their freedom, by studying the law day in and day out. You have those who educate themselves through the means of available books.

The Muslims are one of the strongest forces, if not the strongest in all aspects. They believe in educating the mind and keeping the body strong. They separate themselves from the prison politics. They're not into dealing or using drugs. Nothing that would intoxicate the mind and body is permitted for use among them. What I also noticed about the Muslims is they tend to have a problem with the Nation of Islam Muslims. The Nation of Islam Muslims normally have their own community. They believe in discipline, structure, educating them from the cradle to the grave and teaching Black history, and trying to bring others into Islam. The problem that the two groups of Muslims have is because of the different beliefs concerning the Muslim religion, but they still remain together as one solid mass as Muslim.

The Christian inmates don't involve themselves in anything that has to do with the prison politics, gangs or any violence. Within the Christian group there are a mixture of races. These are the inmates who go to church and proclaim that they are Born Again Christians. That means nothing to any of the prison gangs, especially the Southern Mexicans, the Surenos. If you are a Sureno, you will follow under their rules regardless if you are Christian, or they will lift you off the yard. Also, being a Christian doesn't stop any other race from stabbing them when a race riot occurs. The gangs don't care about any of that. If their race is at war with another race and they are in reach, they will get a knife ran in them without a second thought.

There are many different gangs inside the prisons. The Blacks have the most separation among themselves than any other race of people, but they will all quickly come together when their race is threatened by another race. They are also quick to stab each other.

The Woods, which call themselves the Wood Pile, are a vicious daredevil type of gang. They are very dangerous and suicidal. They have no problem risking it all. They create the most wicked type of prison made knifes ever seen and will attack their target even in front of the cops. They are also known for stabbing officers, and having no problem with doing so. They don't care about the consequences or repercussions. As long as they take out their main targeted victim, all else is fair. They are very strange in their behavior and don't see anything wrong with hugging and kissing each other, sex playing and talking about having sex with another man. Most are drug addicts who love to shoot dope, speed and heroin. Those are the highs of choice. A lot of them love that speed. When they get on that drug they seem to become more creative, sexually active, super hyper, and cruel. There's no telling what they might do once they get to tweaking off that dope, but regardless of all the drugs they may indulge in they still are a dangerous group of people and shouldn't be underestimated, because they are the ones who normally have the best made knifes, and will put them to use immediately. They are also the ones who make prison bombs, have liquid poisons that they put in food and drinks which is undetectable by taste, smell or seen by the naked eye. One thing about the Woods; they will do business with all races. As long as they have the drugs they will spend or trade for items.

The Nazi Skinheads are a totally different bread of white boys. The Woods really don't like them, but they allow them to stay on the lines because they are the same race and it keeps the white race stronger. The Skinheads hate all races. They keep their heads shaved bald and only do business among themselves. They are a wild bunch, very hyper with each other and strict when it comes to dealing with other races. Most of them either have the Nazi Swastika, lightning bolts, or the number 88 tattooed on their body. They are always eager to prove themselves and want to be recognized by others as a tough and vicious gang. They often make examples out of their own race by preying on the weak white boys who come into the prison system who aren't involved in any gang activities. They start by trying to recruit him. It normally ends up that the potential recruit will be reluctant. So the Skins will begin their extortion tactics, and when the money runs dry, they will end up gang raping him and threaten his life. They target the younger white boys who have no ties with any Woods and they carry out their tactics. If there is any type of resistance shown toward them, they will all take flight and try to kill that person. The Skinheads always have problems with the Woods and they tend to fight and stab each other over disagreements. After their little exhibition is over, everything goes right back to normal and there's no grudges between the two. They look at the battle as a training program to keep them ready for the real enemies.

The Southerner Mexicans, Surenos, are united as one gang. There's no distinction with them and the only internal problems they have is when one of them disobeys an order or breaks a rule, or there a snitch coming into the prison that they have to deal with. The Blacks believe that the Southerners are racist, but most Southerners are not. They are forced to follow suit with the politics and rules that have been laid down for them or risk losing their life for going against the grain. They have real strict policies and when a rule is broken there's no slap on the hand; there will be a punishment of some sort. Knowing that there is no room for laws, they just follow all the rules and do what they have to do and are told to do by the southerner who has the authority for that prison. They move around the yard in packs and do everything together. They have a relationship with the whites, and from my observation the Southerners have instilled a little fear into the Woods. I also notice that the Skinheads will not listen to the Southerners, and will take flight (attack) them. The Southerners also love to shoot heroin and smoke speed, but they have a policy that no Southerner will come out to the yard high for any reason. They get high in their cells and remain there until the high is gone. The Southerners are also very sneaky; they are always plotting to do some underhanded sneak attack of some sort. They also don't allow any Mexican homosexuals to walk the mainline with them. If one comes to the yard, they immediately send a hitter to lift him up off the yard. They see homosexuals as disrespect to their race. The Southerners are very respectful to all races, something they take pride in. The Southerners fight with the Blacks, whites, and Northern Mexicans, but also the others.

Those who were not involved in the street life that comes to prison try to stay in the shadows. They mainly keep to themselves and try their best not to be noticed and tend to restrain themselves to the confinement of their cells. They don't look to meet new friends and have very limited conversation, if any, with others. It is the mechanism of staying safe and avoiding life treating situations from the ongoing prison violence. The others are a classified individual whose ethnicity is different than Black, white, or Mexican. They are individuals who are from different countries overseas and islands. They stick together on the prison yards. They don't call themselves a gang and don't have a political structure, they are more of a neutral group who deals and do business with all races, and try not to get involved with the gang activity on the yards. The officers favor the others because they never get into any problems, so they are provided with over ninety percent of the critical jobs in prison, the program clerk positions, cooks, food servers, yard crew, building porters. Normally, when the prison goes on lockdown the others would be the ones not on lockdown after a twenty-four hour emergency assessment period is completed, and then all the critical workers are released to normal program while all the other races remain on lockdown.

The Crips have it the hardest inside the prisons because there are so many different Crip gangs on the yards. When one gets into something on the yard, the institution will lock down all Crip gang members. I also notice that the Crips make their own rules as they feel among them, and they are not all together as a whole.

Every group wants to be the chief, and don't want to follow up under one voice, regardless if that voice could lead them to success. The Crips seem to have an ego problem. Every faction wants to be identified as notorious, tough, and crazy, but they really are mentally challenged. They want the fame and top respect of all gangs, so they normally try to outdo each other when it comes to violent acts. Plus, they are not trustworthy. They care not what you feel about them as long as you recognize they will kill and stomp your face into the ground without any remorse. They are conniving, selfish, disrespectful, could hearted, and out of control, in my opinion. Dealing with a Crip is like sticking your hand into a blazing fire when you know you're going to get burned. All Crip gang members are not Black. You have white boys, Mexicans and other races who are Crips. When they come into the prisons, the administration will classify them as Black regardless of their ethnicity and house them with a Black Crip gang member. The other races don't like to see that and will go to war with the Crips over it. They will make every attempt to try and kill the Crip that's of their race. Issues like that force all the other Blacks to get involved because the Blacks looks at it like an attack on their race and they will not have any other race trying to harm their people. The Crips have some wicked ways and in these prisons they will gang rape one of their own for being a coward and weak. Some are just into having sex with other men and look for a reason to rape someone. The young Crips who come to the prison for the first time seem to become the victims of rape. They come in fearing the unknown and they are willing to give sexual favors to a Crip who they feel could protect them. In the prisons rape is very seldom reported to the officers due to fear of being humiliated, teased, or even killed. The victim will live in a state of denial of the fact that they had been raped. Prison rapes does occur quite often, a lot more than it is reported, and Crips are not the only gangs who carry out such tactics. There are a lot of sick, disgusting, deranged minded people behind these walls. You would never be able to tell just by their appearance and daily actions.

The Northerner Mexicans are laid back and not always uptight or stressed out over anything. They keep a cheerful personality. They are not the type of gang that looks for problems or preys on the weak. They don't involve themselves in homosexual activities, and not into raping their people. They have a hip style, speak street slang and have a similar liking of style and taste as the Blacks.

The Bloods are well respected even by their worst enemies, which are the Crips. The Bloods are a solid structure and well organized. They carry themselves in a respectful manner and are not boastful in their actions and achievements. Bloods seem to be outnumbered by Crips five to one, if not more. The Bloods are mentally stronger, well organized and rational thinkers. They are not quick to place their whole car into a wreck, unless danger presents itself and they must react to protect themselves. I have noticed the Bloods will not rat pack another Blood member if he has an internal problem with another member. He is afforded the opportunity to a head up fight. The Bloods do not tolerate a snitch in their family. They are a vicious gang. Just looking at them or interacting around them they don't seem to be as vicious and violent as they are. If there's a problem with one Blood, you will have a problem with them all, and believe me, they are going to come to take care of business. They don't care how big a gang or group is. If they have a problem with a group, a handful of Bloods would rush the entire group and stab as many people as possible in that crowd. They don't believe in raping, and they will lift you from the yard if you are caught messing around with a homosexual, and will kill you if you rape a Blood. The Bloods are respected by the prison gangs except for the Crips.

The meals in prison are just enough to keep you from starving and having extreme hunger pangs. The remedy to avoid the hunger pangs is to drink a 16oz glass of water before the meal and right after. This method will give you the sensation of feeling full. That's why it's very important to have water stored in your cell if you have the financial means to purchase some. Being caught on lockdown without any canteen, you will feel every moment of that lockdown and most likely will lose a lot of weight.

Prison is not a place to ask other inmates to borrow or give anything, because a price of some sort comes along with everything. The best policy is not to ask for or accept anything from anyone. If you have any artistic skills like drawing, then drawing a few different types of cards can be a way to get the needed items.

Inside the prisons there are a lot of dirty, crooked and vindictive cops. I am speaking from personal knowledge and actual dealings with several crooked officers. I have also seen a lot of things that they do. What everyone must understand is that officers are also human beings who lie and steal and who are egotistic. Although they are correctional officers, that doesn't make them honest, trustworthy or even loyal to their job description. There are correctional officers who bring the drugs into the prison to make the extra money that the inmates give them for smuggling the drugs in. There are also officers who gamble with inmates for money on sports. There are officers who pay inmates to beat down certain inmates that they don't like, and they point out inmates who are snitching.

This is what I learned, seen, viewed and experienced inside the prisons and this is how it is behind the prison walls.

ABOUT THE AUTHOR

The Author is a prolific critic, essayist, poet, and writer of short stories. Additionally, among his many comments about himself that apply to the greater part of his own literary work is an image of a realization, a fragment of great confession to be sure but self-contained of our own nature and surroundings. This book is an autobiography because the author was there in the very midst of the daily danger, violence behind the prison walls and viewed and explored personally what life consist of in the criminal mind. This book goes beyond the reality portrayed on the Home Box Office series OZ.

PRISON SECRETS
Eugene L. Weems

PRISON SECRETS
Eugene L. Weems

EXHIBIT A

MEN'S ADVISORY COUNCIL

199

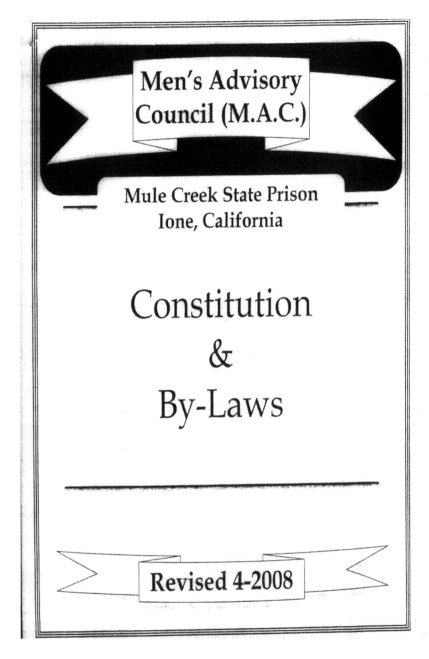

Men's Advisory Council (M.A.C.)

Mule Creek State Prison
Ione, California

Constitution
&
By-Laws

Revised 4-2008

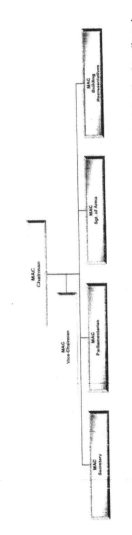

In order for the MAC to be effective there must be a clearly defined Chain-of-Command. All information is gathered by the MAC Building Representatives from the General Population, from the Building Representative suggestions are given to the MAC Secretary for discussion by the Executive Body. Once the Executive Body determines the proper course of action, issues are then given to the appropriate sub-committee chairman to be added to the next agenda. After issues are exhausted by the sub-committees, minutes are typed with the administrations response and disseminated to the Building Representatives by the Secretary for posting in the buildings.

As Building Representatives you are expected to handle issues that are internal to the unit that you represent. As a collective, the four Building Representatives shall address these issues with the Unit Floor Staff. If a resolution cannot be reached, the Senior Representative should contact the Chairman or Vice-Chairman for further action.

All issues from the general population that are covered by a sub-committee must be submitted to the MAC Secretary in writing.

MAC members shall always strive to advance the MAC objectives, work in harmony with other MAC members and sponsors, disregarding differences of race, religion, creed and personality, and complete all projects assigned to them.

MAC members shall maintain the integrity of the MAC membership and are not to utilize the membership to attract people in personal regards or cause embarrassment to the MAC in any matter.

MAC members shall attend all meetings and MAC functions in a punctual fashion, unless properly excused.

MAC members shall always participate in the MAC with honesty and sincerity.

MAC members are required to exercise their voting privileges unless compelled to abstain from voting in order to uphold the integrity of the vote.

ARTICLE IV OFFICERS

Executive Body

There shall be an Executive Body, which shall serve, as the administrative branch of the MAC. This body shall consist of the following:

CHAIRMAN	VICE-CHAIRMAN	SECRETARY	PARLIAMENTARIAN	SERGEANT AT ARMS
(ELECTED)	(APPOINTED)	(ELECTED)	(APPOINTED)	(ELECTED)

There shall be allowed, at the discretion of the Chairman and Vice-Chairman with fifty-one (51%), a simple majority of the General Council concurring and Sponsor approval, (no more than two (2) additional Executive Body Positions with the titles and duties to be determined).

The Chairman shall have the power to appoint any General Council or Honorary Member in good standing to the Vice-Chairman, and Parliamentarian positions, with members of the General Counsel and Executive Body seconding the decision and fifty-one (51%), a simple majority of the General Council concurring.

Each voting member shall have one (1) vote. No member of the Executive Body may simultaneously serve on the General Council.

Terms of Office, all members of the General council may serve a term of two (2) years, at which time he may be re-elected. With the exception of the Vice-Chairman, all appointees may serve a term of two (2) years at which time they may be re-appointed. The Chairman, Vice-Chairman and the Secretary may serve a term of three (3) years after which time they may be re-elected. The Sponsor of the MAC shall be the Facility Captain.

4.1 UNITARY BOARD AND COMPOSITION

There shall be a Unitary Board, which shall serve as the official liaison with the Administration and Warden, as well as the final administrative hierarchy for all the facilities MAC's.

2

There shall be Co-Chairmen of the Unitary Board, consisting of each facilities Chairman. The Unitary Chairman shall be the designated spokesperson/liaison for the Unitary Board, and shall be responsible for preparing and addressing the agendas at the quarterly Warden's meeting as well as other meetings, with said agenda having been agreed upon and signed by the Unitary Board. The positions shall be non-pay, non-assigned and simply a volunteer post in conjunction with that respective individuals assigned position as Chairman for their respective facilities. The Chairman shall have no special authority, nor veto power, over any facility but rather simply serve as the administrative head and liaison for the MAC.

4.2 PROPOSALS AND ADMINISTRATION CONTACT.

All proposals to Administration (i.e. Associate Warden or higher), shall be submitted and endorsed by the Unitary board, after a majority vote in favor thereof, by the board members. No proposal or issue will be addressed by the Administration unless submitted by the board. It is the intent of the MAC and Administration that the board shall serve to ensure that only substantive and genuine issues of importance to the populace are brought to the Administration. Any decision on the board after a majority vote regarding any issue or proposal shall be binding on all Facilities MAC members. No facility will be permitted to have sole control nor will any facility be permitted to veto a majority vote of the board.

4.3 MEETING OF THE BOARD.

The Unitary Board shall serve at the pleasure of the Warden, and meet once monthly at a time and location designated by the Associate Warden, MAC Coordinator, or his/her designee. The Board shall also meet at the direction of the Warden or any other Executive Staff member at such time deemed to be necessary and/or appropriate.

3

PART II
BY-LAWS

SECTION 1 MEMBERSHIP

See Article III, eligibility in the Men's Advisory Council Constitution, pg. 1.

SECTION 2 NOMINATIONS

CHAIRMAN

Nominations for the Chairman shall be taken at the first meeting following the vacancy, except as provided in Section 11, infra. After such nominations are made, the election is conducted at the next General Council meeting. All eligible voting members of the MAC in Good Standing will be permitted to vote.

SECRETARY AND SERGEANT AT ARMS

When a vacancy of the Secretary or Sergeant At Arms occurs, nominations shall be taken at the first meeting of the General Council after the vacancy has occurred.

If any member of the General Council or Executive Body shall be transferred for medical reasons, out to court (OTC), etc., that person shall continue to hold office, subject to monthly evaluations and at the discretion of the Sponsor.

EXECUTIVE BODY

Members of the Executive Body other than the Chairman, Secretary, and Sergeant at Arms shall be appointed by the Chairman and serve at the pleasure of the Chairman with members of the Executive Body seconding the decision and fifty-one (51) percent, a simple majority of the General Council concurring. General Council and Honorary Members in "Good Standing" will be considered for appointment to an Executive Body position. The Chairman, Secretary and the Sergeant At Arms shall always be elected by secret ballot and the Sponsor or his/her designee, if deemed appropriate, will supervise such elections. When a vacancy occurs, nominations for the position of the Chairman, Secretary, and Sergeant At Arms shall be taken at the first meeting following the vacancy, except as provided in Section 4 infra. After such nominations are made, the election shall be completed at the next General Council meeting. All eligible voting members of the MAC in "Good Standing", shall be permitted to vote.

When a vacancy of the Vice-Chairman or Parliamentarian occurs, an appointment shall be made by the Chairman at the first meeting of the General Council after a vacancy has occurred. This appointment must be supported by 51% of the General Council.

Any eligible member of the MAC in "Good Standing", shall be permitted to cast an absentee ballot if the member is excused as a result of 1) Priority Ducat, 2) Medical Lay-in, 3) Work Assignment, 4) etc, as reviewed by the Parliamentarian and approved by the Chairman and Vice-Chairman. The Election Committee shall ensure that the provisions for conducting elections, as set forth in section three (3) above, are followed.

4

Every absentee ballot, upon being cast, shall be placed in an envelope and sealed in the presence of Correctional Staff. The envelope shall remain sealed until the related election is held.

Prior to any vote, a quorum must be established—(General Council membership of 12 plus 1 members; Executive Body of 3 plus 1 members).

GENERAL COUNCIL

REPRESENTATIVES

There shall be four (4) Representatives from each housing unit, Minimum Dorm, and Gymnasium, as follows: one (1) African-American; one (1) Hispanic; one (1) White; one (1) Other Race, for a total of (24) unit representatives. These elected representatives shall constitute the General Council, and each shall have a single vote on the Men's Advisory Council (MAC).

When a vacancy of a unit representative occurs, the Election Committee shall conduct an election by secret ballot in that respective unit. All candidates must reside in the unit in which they are to be nominated and elected. A minimum of 72 hours prior to each election, a standardized MAC "Notice of Election" shall be posted which specifies the vacancy. Provisions will be made to nominate an individual who wishes to run. If there is only one (1) nominee, no election will be held. Election ballots will give the date and time of the election to be held. The Sponsor or his/her designee shall sign every such notice prior to posting.

HONORARY REPRESENTATIVES

There shall be allowed, at the discretion of the Executive Body and with the approval of the Facility Captain, four (4) Honorary Representatives as follows; one (1) African American, one (1) Hispanic, one (1) White, and one (1) Other race, for a total of four (4) Honorary Representatives. These Honorary Representatives shall be non-voting and serve at the pleasure of the Men's Advisory Council.

If the Executive Body agrees, Honorary Representatives may be appointed to the Executive Body as Vice Chairman or Parliamentarian, and may chair standing committees at the discretion of the chairman with fifty-one (51%) percent of the General Council concurring. Only duly elected members of the General Council in good standing will be allowed to run for an elected position on the Executive Body.

Honorary members appointed to Executive Body positions, will not be able to run for any elected positions; to qualify to run for an elected position, they would have to resign their appointed position and be elected as a Building Representative.

SECTION 3 ELECTIONS

The Parliamentarian shall conduct and supervise the election and issue ballots to all members of the ethnic group that is to vote in the Building Unit Representative Election.

5

Following the election and tabulation of the ballots, the Sponsor or his/her designee shall save the notice of election for at least 30 days. Building Correctional Staff will verify and tabulate the ballots once collected by the Election Committee.

SECTION 4 METHOD OF FILLING VACANCIES

When a vacancy of a Building Unit Representative occurs, the Parliamentarian shall conduct an election by secret ballot.

When a vacancy of the Vice-Chairman or Parliamentarian occurs, an appointment shall be made by the Chairman at the first meeting of the General Council after a vacancy has occurred with 51% of the General Council concurring.

SECTION 5 DUTIES OF THE EXECUTIVE BODY

CHAIRMAN

The Chairman shall be an elected position and constitute a full-time work assignment under Penal Code 2933. The Chairman is empowered to appoint and assign members of the MAC to assignments and positions as governed under the By-Laws and Constitution of the Men's, Advisory Council (MAC). The Chairman shall preside over all meetings and be responsible for the agenda of all meetings. The Chairman prior to any meeting shall prepare a written agenda to any regular meeting except in the case of a special or emergency meeting, in which case no formal agenda will be required. The Chairman along with the Vice-Chairman and Secretary shall without fail meet with administrative heads on an as needed basis to express the concerns of the General Population. The Chairman shall also hold weekly Executive Body meetings. The Chairman shall also brief the General Council of all meetings with Administration Heads. The Chairman or his designated representative shall hold the responsibility for the coordination of all standing committees. The Chairman is required to keep the Vice-Chairman and Secretary fully informed of all MAC business, and vice versa. The Chairman shall not sit on the Election Committee.

VICE-CHAIRMAN

The Vice-Chairman shall be an appointed voluntary position and is not a full-time work assignment. The Vice-Chairman is in charge of performing the duties of the Chairman in his absence.

SECRETARY

The Secretary shall be an elected position and constitute a full-time work assignment under Penal Code §2933. The Secretary shall, be present at any meetings with Administrative Department Heads. The Secretary is in charge of performing the duties of the Chairman or Vice-Chairman in either of their absence. When impeachment is pending against the Chairman, the Secretary as the assignment, per Penal Code §2933, *shall perform duties of Chairman*. The Secretary is immediately answerable to the Chairman and or Vice-Chairman. The Secretary shall record all meetings, prepare minutes of all official meetings, maintain a current and complete roster and circulate all official notices. All minutes shall be submitted to the Chairman for review and approved by the sponsor prior to circulation and posting.

6

PARLIAMENTARIAN

The Parliamentarian shall be a voluntary position appointed in accordance to Article 4 and is not a full-time work assignment. The Parliamentarian shall perform all elections and post nomination ballots in the effected units. The Parliamentarian shall be vested with the parliamentary authority. The Parliamentarian shall be the final authority on any procedural point of contention during any official MAC meeting following **ROBERT'S RULES OF ORDER.** The Parliamentarian shall conduct any research necessary for the MAC and shall assist the Secretary in performing his duties as may be deemed necessary by the Secretary.

SERGEANT AT ARMS

The Sergeant At Arms shall be a voluntary position elected in accordance to Article 4 and is not a full-time work assignment. The Sergeant At Arms shall ensure order at all official MAC meetings. The Sergeant At Arms shall also perform other duties as deemed necessary or as directed by the Chairman or Vice-Chairman.

ADDITIONAL EXECUTIVE BODY POSITIONS

Pursuant to Article 4 of the Constitution and By-Laws, any additional titled Executive Body positions shall be voluntary. This position shall be maintained at the discretion of the Chairman with the Vice-Chairman seconding and fifty-one (51%), a simple majority of the General Council concurring. The Chairman and sponsor shall agree upon the duties of any additional Executive Body position. Any additional Executive Body position will be an appointed position.

SECTION 6 MEETINGS

The General Council shall hold monthly meetings on a date designated by the Chairman. Attendance for these meetings are **MANDATORY** for all MAC members not working or who otherwise do not have a priority ducat. In addition to regular meetings, the Chairman or Vice-Chairman may call special meetings with the approval of the Facility Captain (MAC Sponsor). MAC members whose work assignments interfere with the monthly meeting(s) **Shall-Not** be allowed to use ETO or S Time to attend.

The Executive Body shall meet once a week on a date designate by the Chairman.

Standing and Ad-Hoc Committees shall meet bi-weekly or as directed by the Chairman or his designee.

Location of General Council meetings shall be held in a place designated by the MAC Sponsor. Executive Body Meetings may be held wherever it is agreeable to Facility Custodial Staff.

SECTION 7 COMMITTEES

There shall be six (6) Standing Committees on the MAC as follows: Visiting, Food Service, Receiving and Release (R&R), Health Care Services, Canteen, and Mail Room.

7

Committee Chairmen (Standing and Ad-Hoc) shall conduct and coordinate official meetings of the committee of which he is Chairman.

Committee Chairmen shall also provide the General Council with a written report of their activities once each month. Committee Chairman shall report directly to the Executive Body. Chairman, with the majority of the Executive Body concurring shall choose Committee Chairmen.

There shall be Ad-Hoc positions established on an Ad-Hoc basis, as the Executive Body shall determine and with the consent of the Sponsor. The Chairman and Sponsor shall agree upon what the duties of any Ad-Hoc positions consist of until the problem is resolved. Ad-Hoc position/committees shall run for ninety (90) days and can be extended if necessary by the Chairman with the consent of the Sponsor.

All committees shall be comprised of a Chairman and at least two (2) members of ethnic diversity to ensure that all needs will be met. The Executive Body or a quorum shall choose these committees.

Committees shall be restricted to inquire and address problems with respect to the area for which the respective committee has been established, Committee Chairmen shall report to Executive Body and shall brief the General Council at its meeting and supply all reports in writing.

SECTION 8 PARLIAMENTARIAN AUTHORITY

The Parliamentarian shall be vested with the Parliamentary Authority of the MAC. The Parliamentarian shall officiate all meetings of the MAC and shall follow **ROBERT'S RULES OF ORDER** in doing so. The Parliamentarian shall be the final authority of any procedural point of contention during any official MAC meeting.

SECTION 9 EXECUTIVE COMMITTEE

There shall be an Executive Committee of the MAC, consisting of the Executive Body and the Chairman of each Standing and Ad-Hoc Committees.

SECTION 10 ACTIVITY CARDS

·Provisions may be made to issue special activity cards to the Chairman, Vice-Chairman and Secretary of the MAC for their use in Conducting business of the Men's Advisory Council (MAC).

SECTION 11 REMOVAL OF MEMBERS

The Executive Body by a majority vote, for "GOOD CAUSE" showed, may remove any General Council or population member from the MAC. In all cases where a member is removed from the MAC for "GOOD CAUSE", approval shall be required from the sponsor.

8

A General Council Member may upon motion, having been moved and seconded by a member in good standing, recommend removal of any member for good cause as provided in this section. A simple majority vote of the Executive Body concurring shall be required prior to taking the matter before the General Council.

"Good Cause" is demonstrated in all cases where any member, subject to the provisions as outlined in Article 3 herein engages in any activity/behavior that compromises the integrity of the Men's Advisory Council (MAC).

A member of the MAC may be subject to removal from the MAC when said member has sustained a record of unexcused absences from any type of MAC meeting. If a member sustains a record of unexcused absences removal will be at the discretion of the Chairman Three (3) unexcused absences is grounds for removal.

Any member subject to such shall prior to any vote, be given a full and fair opportunity to address the MAC in his own defense. Thereupon, the General Council shall deliberate and finally act by a vote on the question or removal. Without his consent, no member should be tried at the same meeting in which the charges are alleged.

The vote for either removal or retention shall be by secret ballot, or at the discretion of the Chairman, by a show of hands. For removal there must be a majority showing of not less than 51%, a simple majority, of both the Executive Body and General Council.

Prior to any vote a quorum must be established, (General Council of 12 Plus 1; Executive Body of 3 members plus 1).

In all cases of removal, the Chairman is responsible for forwarding the original complaint, minutes of all proceedings of both the Executive Body and the General Council to the sponsor for final approval.

REMOVAL OF THE CHAIRMAN, SECRETARY AND SERGEANT AT ARMS

Any voting member of the MAC in good standing may present a written impeachment petition with clearly specified charges to the Parliamentarian for consideration by the General Council. A copy of the petition shall be served to all members of the General Council, each member of the Executive Body, a copy to the sponsor and a copy posted in each housing unit at least three 3 days prior to the hearing before the General Council.

Upon receipt of a proper impeachment petition, the Parliamentarian shall perform all tasks required to conduct the impeachment process. The Parliamentarian shall work in conjunction with the Sponsor to ensure the integrity of the process is maintained at all times. After service of the impeachment petition as set-forth above, but in no case less than ten (10) days after presentation, the matter shall be debated before the General Council

The member shall prior to any vote, be given a full and fair opportunity to argue his defense before the General Council.

For the purposes of impeachment proceedings, the Parliamentarian and Vice-Chairman shall moderate the debate and discussion of the impeachment proceedings, to ensure

9

that order is upheld throughout the impeachment proceedings. Upon the completion of sufficient debate and discussion as determined by the Vice-Chairman, the matter shall go forth to the MAC for a vote on the question of "Guilty or not guilty".

Upon a finding of guilty to any/all of the charge(s), outlined in the petition the MAC shall proceed to deliberate on the question of "Removal or Retention". A two-thirds ¾, 66% total of the eligible voting members of the MAC, is required to carry any recommendation for removal of the Chairman, Secretary or Sergeant at Arms. The impeachment ballots shall be handled in accordance to the same provisions as set-forth in Section 3, Elections.

If removal carries, the petition and the recommendation shall go to the sponsor for review. If the sponsor agrees with the finding and recommendations, the matter shall go to the MAC Coordinator. Upon review and approval, the matter shall go to the Warden.

The Warden may accept or reject the petition and recommendation, or if deemed appropriate, interview all members involved in the impeachment proceeding. Once any investigation is completed, the MAC will be informed of the Warden's decision. In the case of removal of the Chairman, Secretary, or Sergeant at Arms pursuant to the provisions herein, the Warden shall inform the general population of the action and reason for it.

If the Chairman, Secretary, or Sergeant at Arms should be removed, nominations for the vacant position(s) shall be taken at the first meeting following the vacancy. After such nominations are made, the election shall be completed at the next meeting of the General Council.

REMOVAL OF HONORARY REPRESENTATIVES

If the Chairman and Vice-Chairman concur, their authority may remove any honorary Representative, after a showing of good cause, and the Honorary Representative having had opportunity to address the Chairman and Vice-Chairman. Any such removal shall be immediately documented by the Secretary, with reasons thereof and transmitted to the sponsor. If the Chairman and Vice-Chairman cannot agree, then the removal shall be done in accordance with that of a General Council Representative.

Standing and Ad-Hoc Committee Chairmen and Population Members may be removed from a committee under the same criteria as that of General Council member being removed by the Executive Body.

Executive Body Members (with the exception of the Chairman, Sergeant at Arms and Secretary) are subject to removal under the same procedures as a General Council Member is subject to.

SECTION 12 LEAVE OF ABSENCE

A leave of absence can be requested by any MAC member as needed to the sponsor and its use shall not be abused in any form. The MAC Sponsor thereof must give approval of a leave of absence for valid reason(s), specifically detailing the length.

10

SECTION 13 AMENDMENTS

Proposed amendments and/or modifications to either the Constitution or Bylaws herein must be agreed upon by the Unitary Body of the Men's Advisory Council. The Unitary Body, consisting of the Chairman, Vice Chairman, and Secretary of all three yards has a membership of nine (9) members and any agreement to amend the Constitution or Bylaws must be by a vote of two thirds in agreement, a vote of at least six (6) members. The proposed amendment shall be presented to the sponsor for review and approval. Upon approval of the Warden and sponsor said amendments shall become effective.

11

PART III
ADDENDUM / INFORMATION

D.O.M. §53120.9: ACCOMMODATION:

Issuance of Office Supplies shall require the approval of the appropriate Correctional Captain or the Facility Captain. Office supplies deemed proper and necessary will be furnished through the Captain's office by written request from the Men's Advisory Council (MAC) Chairman.

D.O.M. §53120.13, ARTICLE 3, TITLE 15, INMATE COUNCILS, §3230(b)(4):

Suspension of the Inmate Advisory Committee (MAC). The Warden may suspend the membership of any individual IAC member or the activities of the IAC when there is reason to believe the individual's action or those of the IAC present a threat to the institution security, the safety of person, or is counter productive to the best interests and welfare of the General Population.

D.O.M §53120.14, PRIVILEGES OF THE INMATE ADVISORY COMMITTEE:

Wardens are encouraged to grant such privileges to the IAC, as may seem fair and justified by Staff and Inmate Population for services rendered.

D.O.M §53120.16 CONSTITUTION AND BY-LAWS:

The Men's Advisory Council (MAC) Chairman, Vice-Chairman and Secretary are the members authorized to conduct MAC business in the housing unit, other than their own assigned housing unit, unless specifically authorized by the Facility Lieutenant, Correctional Counselor II or the Facility Captain. The MAC Building representatives are restricted to conducting MAC activities in their assigned housing units only.

D.O.M. §53120.16 MAC BY-LAWS SECTION 11

Removal of Members: Provisions shall be made to remove Building Representatives through recall by their constituents or by administrative order.

D.O.M. §53120.5.2 ELIGIBILITY FOR NOMINATION:

Eligibility for nomination, election as a member of the Inmate Advisory Council (IAC), shall be limited only by the inmate's ability to effectively function in that capacity. Disciplinary violation shall not bar an inmate from nomination, election to or retention on the council unless they reflect behavior detrimental to the effectiveness of the committee.

12

D.O.M. 5§3120.13 SUSPENSION OF INMATE ADVISORY COMMITTEE:

The Warden may suspend the membership of any individual IAC members or the activities of the IAC when there is reason to believe the individuals action or those of the IAC presents a threats to the welfare of the general inmate population.

CCR TITLE 15 §3230

CCR Title15 §3230 (b)(2); A disciplinary infraction shall not necessarily bar an inmate from serving as a council representative unless the infraction is determined by the Warden to be detrimental to the councils effectiveness.

CCR TITLE15 §3230 (b)(3)

A representative's misbehavior while conducting council business or acting under the guise of conducting council business shall be cause for disciplinary or other action.

·······················**END OF CONSTITUTION AND BY-LAWS** ·······················

13

PART IV
CONCLUSION

Submitted on behalf of all Men's Advisory Council (MAC) Chairman's of Mule Creek State Prison (MCSP):

_____
MAC CHAIRMAN
FACILITY 'A'

_____
MAC VICE-CHAIRMAN
FACILITY 'A'

_____
MAC CHAIRMAN
FACILITY 'B'

_____
MAC VICE-CHAIRMAN
FACILITY 'B'

_____
MAC CHAIRMAN
FACILITY 'C'

_____
MAC VICE-CHAIRMAN
FACILITY 'C'

DATE	APPROVED	SIGNATURE
5/20/08	☒ YES ☐ NO	FACILITY 'A' CAPTAIN
5/24/08	☒ YES ☐ NO	FACILITY 'B' CAPTAIN
5/29/08	☒ YES ☐ NO	FACILITY 'C' CAPTAIN
6-2-2008	☒ YES ☐ NO	ASSOCIATE WARDEN CENTRAL SERVICES
6/2/08	☒ YES ☐ NO	ASSOCIATE WARDEN PROGRAM AND HOUSING
6/3/08	☒ YES ☐ NO	CHIEF DEPUTY WARDEN (A)
6/4/08	☒ YES ☐ NO	WARDEN

14

214

Facility "A" Men's Advisory Council

Date: December 10, 2009
To: Facility "A" General population
From: Men's Advisory Council

Dear population members,

Last year the new Integrated Housing Program (I.H.P.) was implemented. The program eliminated the ability to pick your own cellmate or get any kind of convenience move. Major problems have erupted at prisons starting to enforce the program. The Men's Advisory Council decided to draft a proposal requesting specific changes to I.H.P. We believed that inmates could accept "kick-outs" from Ad-Seg and orientation, so long as a convenience move to pick your own cellmate was allowed after a reasonable period of time. CHairman Prince and I presented the proposal on behalf of all three yards at an emergency Warden's meeting. Warden Martel agreed to foward our proposal to Headquarters. Several top officials from Headquarters traveled to Mule Creek to discuss the subject. They asked us to thank the population for cooperating with I.H.P. and agreed to seriously consider our proposed changes to the program. We are very pleased to announce that our modifications were accepted by Headquarters and the resulting memorandum changing I.H.P. to allow convenience moves is posted in all the units. The administration began slowly losening cellmove requirements months ago in anticipation of the new changes. Nevertheless, read the memorandum carefully to understand the conditions, waiting period, etc. This victory in altering I.H.P. procedures will significantly improve the lives of inmates at every prison in the state.

Last winter we secured approval for the general population to be allowed the nylon winter jackets. We are the only prison without snowfall to be granted such approval. The cost involved means it will take a few years for enough jackets to be ordered to supply every inmate on all three yards. When the nylon winter jackets are out of stock, the laundry is ONLY obligated to give you a denim jacket. Do not 602 the jacket issue. 602s will only succeed in ruining something we fought hard to achieve. We want to thank Supervisor Pam Baker for her patience and diligence, and for continuing to order jackets. Our E.S.P.N. proposal is now at Headquarters. The Warden is personally involved in the talks with them. The process takes time and we do not expect to hear anything until late January. M.A.C. at other prisons have contacted us asking to see our E.S.P.N. proposal. We feel Mule Creek is uniquely positioned for approval and have asked them to be patient. E.S.P.N. approval for other prisons will be easier if we succeed first, just as our victory years ago in gaining permission for Edited-R videos opened the door for prisons across the state. A few more updates: the new digital antenna is now up over the media center, our request for an additional food sale each year was approved and we thank Mr. Laituri for allowing two more food items.

Our thanks to Captain Harrington for starting the painting of cell doors and
railings earlier than expected. We also thank Sgt. White for continuing to make
sure the morning yard gets out on time and successfully implementing the
dual-building release method. We applaud the soccer and football leagues for
working together to share the field during the week to accommodate multiple
practices.

Sincerely,

R.L. Harrington, Captain
Reviewed by: Date: 12/4/03

L. Menendez.
Executive Vice-Chairman

T.E. Prince
Executive Chairman

PRISON SECRETS
Eugene L. Weems

EXHIBIT B

115 RULES VIOLATION

199

SENT TO RECORDS ON 08-28-09   CASE: N/A

STATE OF CALIFORNIA   DEPARTMENT OF CORRECTIONS

RULES VIOLATION REPORT

CDC NUMBER	INMATE'S NAME		RELEASE/BOARD DATE	INST.	HOUSING NO.	LOG NO.
T-40463	WEEMS	[BLK]		MCSP	AG-155M	A-08-09-137
VIOLATED RULE NO(S).	SPECIFIC ACTS			LOCATION	DATE	TIME
CCR §3024	PUBLISHING BOOK FOR SALE			FACILITY "A"	08-25-09	0930 HOURS

CIRCUMSTANCES

On August 25, 2009, at approximately 0930 hours, I conducted an interview with inmate WEEMS, T-40463, AG-155M, regarding a book he had published with Trafford Publishing. The book: "United We Stand A Tribute To The American Fallen Heroes Of The War On Terrorism" was released on July 4, 2009.

I was contacted by the Mail Room Supervisor R. Garcia who had discovered inmate WEEMS was sending fliers to individuals in the community. These fliers gave a description of the author inmate WEEMS and promoted his book, along with a contact number for Trafford Publishing and several websites where the reader could purchase the book for the amount of $14.95. See Attached.

[RULE VIOLATION REPORT CONTINUED ON CDCR-115C]

REPORTING EMPLOYEE (Typed Name and Signature)		DATE	ASSIGNMENT	ROD'S
E. HOBBS, CORRECTIONAL SERGEANT			ISU	3A/SU/H
REVIEWING SUPERVISOR'S SIGNATURE	DATE	☐ INMATE SEGREGATED PENDING HEARING		
A. GREEN, CORRECTIONAL SERGEANT, ISU	8/21/09			
	DATE		LOC.	
CLASSIFIED	OFFENSE DIVISION:	DATE	CLASSIFIED BY (Typed Name and Signature)	HEARING REFERRED TO
☐ ADMINISTRATIVE	F	9/2/09	E. Pahul LT	☐ HO ☒ SHO ☐ SC ☐ FC
☒ SERIOUS				

COPIES GIVEN INMATE BEFORE HEARING

| ☒ CDC 115 | BY: (STAFF'S SIGNATURE) | DATE | TIME | TITLE OF SUPPLEMENT | |
| ☐ INCIDENT REPORT LOG NUMBER: | BY: (STAFF'S SIGNATURE) | DATE | TIME | BY: (STAFF'S SIGNATURE) | DATE | TIME |

HEARING

REFERRED TO ☐ CLASSIFICATION ☐ BPT/NAEA

ACTION BY: (TYPED NAME)		SIGNATURE	DATE	TIME
REVIEWED BY: (SIGNATURE)	DATE	CHIEF DISCIPLINARY OFFICER'S SIGNATURE	DATE	
R. L. HARRINGTON, FACILITY "A" CAPTAIN		W. KNIPP, ASSOCIATE WARDEN		
☐ COPY OF CDC 115 GIVEN INMATE AFTER HEARING		BY: (STAFF'S SIGNATURE)	DATE	TIME

CDC 115 (7/88)

STATE OF CALIFORNIA
RULES VIOLATION REPORT - PART C

DEPARTMENT OF CORRECTIONS
PAGE ___ OF ___

CDC NUMBER	INMATE'S NAME	LOG NUMBER	INSTITUTION	TODAY'S DATE
T-40463	WEEMS	A-08-09-137	MCSP	09-20-09

☐ SUPPLEMENTAL ☑ CONTINUATION OF: ☐ 115 CIRCUMSTANCES ☐ HEARING ☐ IE REPORT ☐ OTHER ___

HEARING PREPARATION:
Mental Health, DDP, DPP and T.A.B.E. score rosters were verified. TABE score is above 4.0.
Inmate WEEMS IS NOT a participant in the Mental Health Services Delivery System.
The SHO DOES NOT elect to assign a Staff Assistant as inmate WEEMS's actions WERE NOT considered "Bizarre, unusual, or uncharacteristic behavior.
Inmate WEEMS DOES NOT DEMONSTRATE impairment in his ability to comprehend the nature of the charges/disciplinary process.
Inmate WEEMS appeared before the Senior Hearing Officer on 09-20-09, at approximately 1000 hours.
Inmate WEEMS stated that he was in good health and that he DOES NOT have a disability (vision/hearing), which requires staff assistance. He written, hearing or sign language interpreter, and is ready to proceed with the hearing.
All written reports considered as evidence HAVE been issued to inmate WEEMS in this matter.
The reports WERE issued at least 24 hours in advance of this hearing.
The reports inmate WEEMS has received includes: CDCR-115, 115A, CDCR-115C continuation, and photocopy flyer.
All time constraints HAVE been met.

DISTRICT ATTORNEY REFERRAL:
This matter WAS NOT referred to the District Attorney.

ASSIGNMENT OF STAFF ASSISTANT/INVESTIGATIVE EMPLOYEE (CDCR-115-A):
Inmate WEEMS DOES NOT MEET the Criteria per CCR §3315(d)(2) for assignment of Staff Assistant.
Inmate WEEMS DOES NOT MEET the Criteria per CCR §3315(d)(1) for assignment of Investigative Employee

INMATE WEEMS'S STATEMENT:
Inmate WEEMS was read and acknowledged understanding of the charge filed against him.
Inmate WEEMS pleads NOT GUILTY to the written charge.
Inmate WEEMS stated, "This is not a business dealing. I'm not trying to make a profit. One hundred percent of the money made on the book goes to support the troops and their families. Sergeant Hobbs called the publisher and did the research to make sure what I was saying was true. He told me if it wasn't I would be getting a lot more than a 115. Also, the write-ups I got at Salinas were Administrative and that was a couple of years ago. That was a different situation and both those write ups were for the same deal. This is different, all the money from this book is going to support the troops."

ADDITIONAL EVIDENCE:
Inmate Weems also provided the SHO with a copy of Penal Code section 2601, which states in part: "Powers of director of corrections are broad but not unlimited and director may not arbitrarily infringe upon prisoner's right to have manuscript... Prisoner has right both to own and to sell his manuscripts." Inmate Weems asserted the penal code gives him the right to promote and sell the book. Title 15 Section 3024 (a) states, "Inmates shall not engage

SIGNATURE OF WRITER D. CHAMBERS, CORRECTIONAL LIEUTENANT, SHO	DATE SIGNED 09-20-09	
☐ COPY OF CDC 115-C GIVEN TO INMATE	GIVEN BY: (Staff's Signature)	DATE SIGNED	TIME SIGNED

CDC 115-C (5/95)

OSP 07 101947

219

STATE OF CALIFORNIA

RULES VIOLATION REPORT - PART C

DEPARTMENT OF CORRECTIONS

PAGE___ OF___

CDC NUMBER	INMATE'S NAME	LOG NUMBER	INSTITUTION	TODAY'S DATE
T-40463	WEEMS	A-05-09-137	MCSP	09-20-09

☐ SUPPLEMENTAL ☑ CONTINUATION OF ☐ 115 CIRCUMSTANCES ☐ HEARING ☐ IE REPORT ☐ OTHER____

actively in a business or profession except as authorized by the institution head or as provided in Section 3104. For the purpose id this section, a business is denied as any revenue generation or profit making activity." The SBO finds CCR 3024 (a) does not arbitrarily infringe on inmate Weems' right to own and sell his manuscript (book), only that it requires authorization by the institution head (Warden or designee). Inmate Weems did not obtain authorization.

WITNESSES/EVIDENCE:
Inmate WEEMS DID NOT request witnesses present at the hearing as indicated on the CDCR-115-A.

FINDINGS: The SHO finds inmate WEEMS Guilty of CCR 3024 "Publishing a Book for Sale (Unauthorized Business Dealings)." This finding is based upon the following preponderance of evidence:
1) The CDCR-115 report authored by Sergeant E Hobbs, which states on August 25, 2009, at approximately 0930 hours, he conducted an interview with inmate Weems (T-40463) regarding a book inmate Weems had published with Trafford Publishing titled "United We Stand A Tribute To The American Fallen Heroes Of the War On Terrorism." The book was released on July 4, 2009. Sergeant Hobbs had been contacted by MCSP Mail Room Supervisor R. Garcia who had discovered inmate Weems had been sending flyers to individuals in the outside community giving a description of the book, the author, and listing websites the book could be bought at for the amount of $14.95. Inmate Weems had previously been found guilty of the same offense on January 16, 2007 and May 10, 2007 while at Salinas Valley State Prison for promoting a book he had written entitled "Prison Secrets." Sergeant Hobbs notes Title 15 section 3024 (a) prohibits inmates from engaging in revenue generating or profit making activity.

2) The copy of flyers that inmate Weems was sending to outside community. The SHO finds the flyers, which contain descriptions of the book and inmate Weems and which lists where the book can be purchased and the purchase price, constitutes a revenue generating activity as prohibited in Title 115 section 3024 (a).

DISPOSITION:
This RVR was originally classified as a Division "F" Offense; however, the SHO elects to reduce it to an Administrative Level CDCR-115.

Reason for Reduction: Progressive Discipline.

ASSESSED 40 hours of extra duty to be completed by October 20, 2009 under the supervision of "A" Gym Staff, Second Watch.

Inmate WEEMS was counseled and reprimanded.

SIGNATURE OF WRITER D. CHAMBERS, CORRECTIONAL LIEUTENANT, SHO		DATE SIGNED 09-20-09	
☐ COPY OF CDC 115-C GIVEN TO INMATE	GIVEN BY: (Staff's Signature)	DATE SIGNED	TIME SIGNED

CDC 115-C (5/95)

OSP 07 101947

STATE OF CALIFORNIA　　　　　　　　　　　　　　　　　　　　　　　DEPARTMENT OF CORRECTIONS

RULES VIOLATION REPORT - PART C　　　　　　　　　　　　　　　　PAGE___ OF___

CDC NUMBER	INMATE'S NAME	LOG NUMBER	INSTITUTION	TODAY'S DATE
T-40463	WEEMS	A-06-09-137	MCSP	09-20-09

☐ SUPPLEMENTAL ☑ CONTINUATION OF: ☐ 115 CIRCUMSTANCES ☐ HEARING ☐ IE REPORT ☐ OTHER_____

Inmate WEEMS, was advised of his right to appeal the findings and/or disposition of the hearing, pursuant to CCR §3084.1, and also advised that he would receive a complete copy upon final audit by the Chief Disciplinary Officer. The review and signature of the Chief Disciplinary Officer affirms, reverses, or modifies this disciplinary action and/or Credit Forfeiture.

SHO NOTES: On September 20, 2009, at approximately 1000 hours, I conducted the hearing in regards to RVR Log #A-06-09-137 issued to inmate Weems (T-40463), for the specific act of "Publishing a book for Sale." Inmate Weems entered a plea of "Not Guilty" and stated, "This is not a business dealing. I'm not trying to make a profit. One hundred percent of the money made on the book goes to support the troops and their families. Sergeant Hobbs called the publisher and did the research to make sure what I was saying was true. He told me if it wasn't I would be getting a lot more than a 115. Also, the write-ups I got at Salinas were Administrative and that was a couple of years ago. That was a different situation and both those write ups were for the same deal. This is different, all the money from this book is going to support the troops." The SHO finds inmate Weems guilty and elects to reduce the charge to Administrative in accordance with progressive discipline.

SIGNATURE OF WRITER	DATE SIGNED
B. CHAMBERS, CORRECTIONAL LIEUTENANT, SHO	
GIVEN BY: (Staff's Signature)	DATE SIGNED	TIME SIGNED

☐ COPY OF CDC 115-C GIVEN TO INMATE

CDC 115-C (5/95)　　　　　　　　　　　　　　　　　　　　　　　　OSP 07 101947

PRISON SECRETS
Eugene L. Weems

EXHIBIT C

CORRESPONDENCE

199

State of California

Department of Corrections and Rehabilitation

Memorandum

Date: August 25, 2009

To: Inmate Prince, C-58784
A1-235L

Subject: **PROPOSAL FOR DONATIONS TO PURCHASE BOOKS**

This memorandum is in response to your letter sent to Warden Martel asking for approval for solicitation of the inmate population on Facility A for donation to purchase books, "United We Stand." Based on the nature of your correspondence this matter was referred to my office for review.

After reviewing the information you included in your letter, I need you to provide additional specific information pertaining the process on the following:

- What assurance are there that all the proceeds from the sale of the books are going to "college scholarships" and "care packages" for American Soldiers. I have called the publisher, but they failed to return my call.

- If an inmate contributes to the donation drive but does not contribute the full purchase price of the book, does he get a copy of the book?

- Why can't inmates purchase the book on an individual basis instead of "pooling" the money through a long, involved donation drive process?

- If approved, what are the timeframes for the donation drive? Who will be coordinating the drive? How will the inmate population be solicited?

Please respond in writing to me with an outline detailing in specific terms the above mentioned issues.

R. LAITURI
Correctional Counselor II
Program Supervisor

Cc: W. Knipp

223

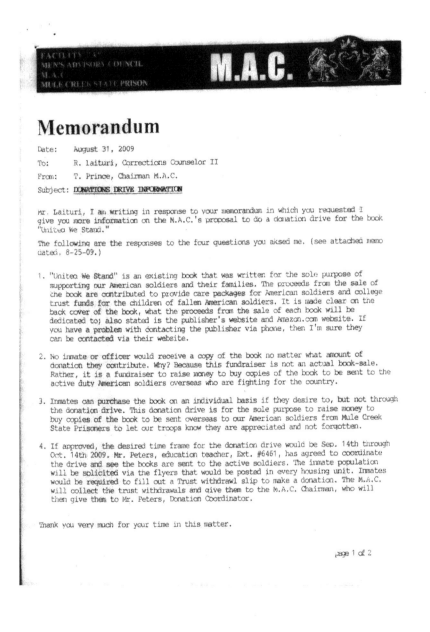

Memorandum

Date: August 31, 2009

To: R. laituri, Corrections Counselor II

From: T. Prince, Chairman M.A.C.

Subject: DONATIONS DRIVE INFORMATION

Mr. Laituri, I am writing in response to your memorandum in which you requested I give you more information on the M.A.C.'s proposal to do a donation drive for the book "United We Stand."

The following are the responses to the four questions you aksed me. (see attached memo dated. 8-25-09.)

1. "United We Stand" is an existing book that was written for the sole purpose of supporting our American soldiers and their families. The proceeds from the sale of the book are contributed to provide care packages for American soldiers and college trust funds for the children of fallen American soldiers. It is made clear on the back cover of the book, what the proceeds from the sale of each book will be dedicated to; also stated is the publisher's website and Amazon.com website. If you have a problem with contacting the publisher via phone, then I'm sure they can be contacted via their website.

2. No inmate or officer would receive a copy of the book no matter what amount of donation they contribute. Why? Because this fundraiser is not an actual book-sale. Rather, it is a fundraiser to raise money to buy copies of the book to be sent to the active duty American soldiers overseas who are fighting for the country.

3. Inmates can purchase the book on an individual basis if they desire to, but not through the donation drive. This donation drive is for the sole purpose to raise money to buy copies of the book to be sent overseas to our American soldiers from Mule Creek State Prisoners to let our troops know they are appreciated and not forgotten.

4. If approved, the desired time frame for the donation drive would be Sep. 14th through Oct. 14th 2009. Mr. Peters, education teacher, Ext. #6461, has agreed to coordinate the drive and see the books are sent to the active soldiers. The inmate population will be solicited via the flyers that would be posted in every housing unit. Inmates would be required to fill out a Trust withdrawl slip to make a donation. The M.A.C. will collect the trust withdrawals and give them to the M.A.C. Chairman, who will then give them to Mr. Peters, Donation Coordinator.

Thank you very much for your time in this matter.

page 1 of 2

page 2 of 2

T.E Prince
Executive Chairman
Men's Advisory Council

J. Iefsaker, OT
Facility "A"

Date_____reviewed.

PRISON SECRETS
Eugene L. Weems

EXHIBIT D

CANTEEN ORDER FORM

199

VITAMINS & OVER-THE-COUNTER MEDICATIONS / PREPARATIONS	
Antifungal Cream	1.95 I
Aspirin	1.20 I‡
Good Sense Muscle Rub	1.35 I
Good Sense Decongestant	1.75 I
Sugar Free Cough Drops	1.80 I
Hydrocortisone Cream	2.20 I
Ibuprofen	2.25 I‡
Medicated Chest Rub	2.25 I
Multi-Vitamins Natural Grocers	2.60 I
Tums Ex 3-roll pack	2.85 I
Protein Tablets	6.30 I
Vitamin C	2.35 I
Vitamin E	2.10 I
Ultra Amino Acid	7.45 I

COSMETIC HAIR CARE		
Balsam Conditioner	◎	1.75
Balsam Shampoo	◎	1.25
Blue Magic Conditioner		2.40
Cream Relax Kit		10.00
Dandruff Shampoo	◎	1.45
Hair Pick		.55
Moisturizing Lotion	◎	1.30
Murray's Pomade		2.95
Pocket Hair Brush (Palm Brush)		.30
Spike It Gel		1.85
Three Flowers Pomade		3.00
Grey Be-Rag		1.15

TOILETRIES PERSONAL ITEMS		
Afta After Shave		3.40
Anti-Perspirant Fresh	◎	2.50
Aquafresh Sensitive		3.75
Bic Two Blade Shavers 10/pk		2.65 H
Body Powder	◎	1.40
Colgate Gel	◎	2.40
Oxygen 3 in 1	◎	3.40
Dental Flosser		1.70
Deodorant Ocean Surf	◎	2.90 I
Disposable Razor		.20 H
Irish Spring Soap	◎	.80
Ivory Bar Soap	◎	.55
Shave Cream Tube		1.45
Medicated Skin Cream		1.25
Effergrip		4.55 I
Fingernail Clippers		.50 H
Denture Cleanser		2.80 I
Men's Perfumed Oil		5.45 I
Mouthwash		3.00 I
Toenail Clippers		.90 H
Tone Soap	◎	1.05 I
Toothbrush (Soft Only)		.60 I
Toothbrush Cap		.29 I

MISCELLANEOUS SUNDRY	
Cap (Light Gray Only)	5.55 I
Chapel Lip Balm	.90 I
Cotton Handkerchief	.80 I
Cotton Swabs	.95 *I
Ear Buds	3.00 N I
Reading Glasses	3.45 I
1.5, 2.0, 2.5, 3.0	
Heavenly Sunglasses	3.75 I
KD Sunglasses	3.80 I
Mirror (6" x 4.5")	2.85 I
Shoe Polish Brown	3.20 I
Shower Shoes (XL Only)	.90 I
Soap Box	.85 I
Tide Laundry Detergent	7.60 I
Wash Cloth	.85 I
Sun Detergent	1.80 I
Weight Gloves	4.00 N I

GREETING CARDS	
Thinking of You / Sweetheart	.70 I
Thinking of You / General	.70 I
Birthday / Sweetheart	.70 I
Birthday / General	.70 I
Birthday / Child	.70 I

STATIONERY ITEMS	
1 Set of 4 44 cent Stamps	1.76 I
No Single Stamps Sold	
1 Set of 5 Envelopes	.19 I
Envelope 9 x 12	.15 I
Expanding Envelope	1.85 I
Large Tablet (Legal)	1.05 I
Legal Paper	1.13 I
Pen, Black	.35 I
Pencil 2.5	.20 I
Photo Album	2.25 I
Webster's Dictionary	1.95 I
Writing Tablet (Small)	.90 I

MISCELLANEOUS HOUSEHOLD ITEMS	
Battery, "AA"	.40 I
Battery, "AAA"	.40 I
Battery, "C"	1.35 I
Battery, "D"	1.10 I
Canteen Bag - 30 x 48	5.00 I
Can Openers (one only)	1.35 I
Cereal Bowl with Lid	1.50 I
Dish Soap	1.70 I
Mug with Lid	3.15 I
Spoon, Zylon, 6 - 1/2	.75 I
TV Cable Splitter	3.15 I
Splitter Adapter	1.10 I
TV Coaxial Cable 6'	3.95 I
Utility Hook	1.35 I
Water Bottle	1.80 I

JANUARY

NO BAGS PROVIDED WITH PURCHASE

JANUARY 2011

FACILITY A, B, C, & MINIMUM

FIRST DRAW	00-33	January 4, 2010
SECOND DRAW	34-66	January 11, 2011
THIRD DRAW	67-99	January 18, 2012

FEBRUARY 2011

FACILITY A, B, C, & MINIMUM

FIRST DRAW	00-33	FEBRUARY 8, 2011
SECOND DRAW	34-66	FEBRUARY 15, 2011
THIRD DRAW	67-99	FEBRUARY 22, 2011

CLOSED LAST WEEK OF THE MONTH

Laura Brown
Prison Canteen Manager II
Business Services Division

Tami Somara
Correctional Business Manager I
Business Services Division

MCSP Canteen (Rev 7/28/10)

JANUARY 2011 CANTEEN ORDER FORM

Name _____ CDCR# _____

Housing Unit _____ Cell Number _____

If an item you requested is out of stock, do you authorize substitution of a similar item? Yes ☐ No ☐

- All Sales Final - NO EXCEPTIONS
- Prices, sizes, brands, subject to change without notice
- Only current canteen lists accepted
- Only use black or blue ink pen
- Canteen closed each month for inventory
- Canteen closed on all state-approved holidays
- Disruptive individuals will be refused service

N = New Item A = Not Sold in A-Canteen * = Price Decrease Ø = Contract Item D = Discontinued After Stock is Sold
S = Special Item TO = Temporarily Out of Stock ** = Price Increase E = Not Sold to EOP Inmates I = Not Sold to Infirmary Inmates

SOUPS

Chicken Noodles	Ø	.35 I
Hot Chili Noodles	Ø	.25 I
Picante Beef Noodles	Ø	.25 I

CHIPS - CRACKERS - POPCORN

Barbecue Chips	Ø	2.00 I
Cheese Crunchy	Ø	1.65 I
Sour Cream & Onion	Ø	2.00 I
Chili Cheese Corn Chips	Ø	1.65 I
Jalapeño Chips	Ø	2.00 I
Nacho Chips	Ø	2.60 I
Pork Rinds	Ø	1.65 I
Flour Tortillas 8"		1.30 I
Corn Tortillas		.80 I
Saltine Crackers	Ø	2.00 I
Cheese Crackers	Ø	2.15 I
Snack Crackers	Ø	2.50 I
Cheese Popcorn		1.30 I
Peanuts, Dry Roasted Tea		1.40 I

CANDY

M & M Peanut	Ø	.90 I
M & M Plain	Ø	.90 I
Milky Way	Ø	.90 I
Nutrageous Candy Bar	Ø	.90 I
Reeses Peanut Butter Cups	Ø	.90 I
Snickers	Ø	.90 I
Snickers With Almonds	Ø	.90 I
Twix	Ø	.90 I
Tootsie Roll Midgets	Ø	.06 I
Tootsie Roll Pops	Ø	.15 AI

COOKIES & PASTRIES

Peanut Butter Cookies	Ø	1.35 I
Raspberry Cookies	Ø	1.40 I
Chocolate Chip Cookies	Ø	1.25 I
Chocolate Cream Cookies	Ø	1.35 I
Oatmeal Cookies	Ø	1.25 I
Duplex Cream Cookies	Ø	1.35 I
Chocolate Drizzle Danish		.90 NI
Honey Bun		.90 I
Muffin, Banana Nut		1.05 I
Muffin, Blueberry		1.05 I
Chocolate Cup Cakes		1.05 I

ICE CREAM

Carnation Ice Cream Sandwich		.70 I
Ice Tickle		.40 I
Butter Pecan Ice Cream Dreyers		2.30 I
Chocolate Ice Cream Dreyers		2.30 I
Vanilla Ice Cream		2.30 I
Maxx Chocolate Peanut Butter		2.95 I
Maxx Butterfinger Dreyers		2.95 I
Maxx Jowa Moth Dreyers		2.95 I
Maxx Drum Stick Dreyers		2.95 I

NO SPOONS PROVIDED WITH PURCHASE

SODAS

Pepsi Cola 12oz	Ø	.55 I
Diet Dr. Pepper 12oz	Ø	.55 I
Mountain Dew 12oz	Ø	.55 I
Mug Root Beer 12oz	Ø	.55 I

MISCELLANEOUS BEVERAGES

Coffee Creamer	Ø	1.80 I
Folgers 3oz		7.25 I
Freeze-Dried Coffee 3oz	Ø	2.70 I
Maje Instant Coffee 8oz		4.90 N
Hot Cocoa 8-pack S/F		2.20 I
Powdered Milk		4.20 I
Strums Kiwi Strawberry		4.05 I
Strums Lemonade		4.05 I
Sweet Thing Aspartame	Ø	1.50 I
Tea Bags		1.80 I
Tang, Sugar Free Sports Drink		2.95 I

SPICES

Adobo Seasoning	Ø	.90 I
Bacon Bits Imitation	Ø	.75 I
Cinnamon	Ø	.75 I
Crushed Peppers	Ø	.75 I
Garlic Powder	Ø	.90 I
Lemon Juice		.75 I
Minced Onions	Ø	1.00 I
Salt & Pepper		1.80 I
Seasoned Salt	Ø	.75 I
Vegetable Flakes		1.35 I

FOOD ITEMS - CONDIMENTS

Beans, Instant Refried 8oz	Ø	1.30 I
Beef Stew / Pouch	Ø	1.85 I
Cereal Srowlers		3.10 NI
Cheese Cheddar 14 oz	Ø	2.06 I
Cheese Habanero 14oz	Ø	2.00 I
Chili No Beans / Pouch	Ø	1.50 I
Chili With Beans / Pouch	Ø	1.50 I
Extra Virgin Olive Oil		3.25 I
Hot and Spicy Sausage		1.75 I
Hot Beef Stick		1.20 I
Hot Beef & Jalapeno Cheese Stick		1.20 I
Hot Sauce	Ø	.75 I
Garlic Hot Sauce	Ø	2.70 I
Jack Mack / Pouch		2.00 I
Macaroni and Cheese		.85 I
Mackerel Fillet / Pouch	Ø	1.00 I
Mayonnaise 11oz	Ø	2.30 I
Meatballs	Ø	2.20 I
Mixed Vegetables		1.15 I
Oatmeal Instant (Flavored)	Ø	2.50 I
Olives, Green / Pouch		1.60 I
Oyster Smoked / Pouch	Ø	1.06 I
Peanut Butter	Ø	2.25 I
Peppers, Jalapeno	Ø	1.80 I
Peppers, Yellow	Ø	1.80 I
Picante Sauce	Ø	1.00 I
Pickle, Hot / Pouch	Ø	.80 I
Pickle, Kosher / Pouch	Ø	.80 I
Rice, Pre-Cooked	Ø	.85 I
Roast Beef / Pouch	Ø	3.50 TO
Salmon / Pouch	Ø	1.40 I
Sardines / Pouch	Ø	.85 I
Shredded Beef	Ø	3.50 NI
Soy Sauce 5oz	Ø	1.15 I
Spam / Pouch	Ø	1.40 I
Tuna / Pouch	Ø	1.10 I
Vienna Sausage / Pouch	Ø	1.85 I

CANNED FOOD PRODUCTS

Beef Stew	Ø	2.30 AI
Chili No Beans	Ø	2.15 AI
Chili With Beans	Ø	1.50 AI
Meatballs	Ø	2.75 AI
Menudo Hot	Ø	2.10 AI
Olives	Ø	1.90 AI
Roast Beef	Ø	3.60 AI
Tuna	Ø	1.20 AI
Spam	Ø	3.25 AI
Chicken Vienna Sausage	Ø	.70 AI

Eugene L. Weems

ABOUT THE AUTHOR

Eugene L. Weems is the bestselling author of *United We Stand* and award winning author of *Prison Secrets*. Weems is co-author of *The Other Side of the Mirror, Head Gamez, and Players Exposed* and *Bound by Loyalty*.

The former kick boxing champion is a producer, model, philanthropist, and founder of No Question Apparel and Inked Out Beef books. He is from Las Vegas, Nevada.

UNITED WE STAND

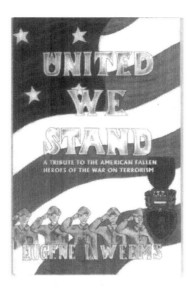

A TRIBUTE TO THE AMERICAN FALLEN HEROES OF THE WAR ON TERRORISM

By Eugene L. Weems

United We Stand is a beautiful collection of inspirational artwork and passion-filled poetry created as a living tribute to the American troops who have made the ultimate sacrifice for our country in the war against terrorism.

100% of the proceeds from this book will be contributed to provide care packages for the active duty troops who remain engaged in the war overseas and provide college scholarship trust funds for the children of our American fallen heroes.

$14.95   95 pgs   6x9 Paperback   ISBN: 978-1-4251-9130-6

Head Gamez

Eugene L. Weems
Timothy R. Richardson

When a team of four beautiful but deadly assassins are given covert assignments to track down and eliminate Hip Hop's biggest Gangsta Rappers....

"Who gets hit next in this crazy game of killers for hire?"

The world may never find the right man, because sometimes the best man for the job is a woman.

14.95   325 pgs   6x9 Paperback   ISBN: 978-0-9840456-1-7

THE OTHER SIDE OF THE MIRROR

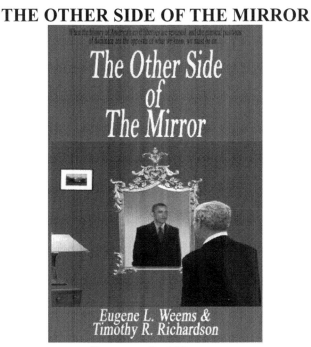

Eugene L. Weems
Timothy R. Richardson

What if Black was White and White was Black?
Could there really be an alternate universe out there?

Join this array of multi-layered characters, each with their own secrets to protect, in their attempts to solve the mystery of the missing President. This story of political intrigue, sexual innuendo and blatant back-stabbing will shock, mystify and intrigue you, with a surprise ending that will leave you breathless!

$14.95   303 pgs   6x9 Paperback   ISBN: 978-0-9840456-0-0

JACKSON RANCH RESCUE Feline Sanctuary is a nonprofit organization which aids abused, abandoned, injured and neglected felines.

We rescue animals in distress whenever an urgent call is received. Our volunteers work with feral cats as we try to acclimate them to human so they can be adopted. We have had much success in this area.

Your generous support and assistance is needed. You can help by making a charitable contribution toward the food, shelter and veterinary care, including spay and neuter costs, for these beautiful animals. Your contribution is tax deductible and will be gratefully received.

THANK YOU FOR YOUR GENEROSITY

242

Players Exposed: How men manipulate women

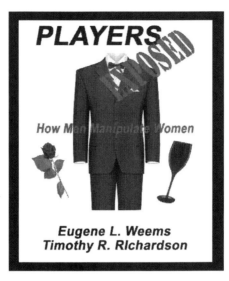

Players exposed is the first book of its kind that reveals the methods used by men to manipulate woman. Here you will find the truth on how men entrap them in love and romantic adventures; using snares of empty promises, and hopeless possibilities. Learn their approach to infiltrating dating sites, pen-pal sites, social networking sites, chat lines, and even the subconscious thoughts.

This extraordinary virtual reality perspective permits an entry into a world the reader would never have been privileged to explore without this book. Learn the signs, and avoid them in this "tell-all-book." Players exposed invites you to familiarize yourself with the persuasive language and deceptive arts of con that leave woman vulnerable and misused.

Even the most intelligent of woman find themselves a victim to the charm and word play in the psychological whirlwind of persuasion used by men for personal gain.

Learn to identify the so-called player at "Hello" and be the first to say "good-bye." Don't become or continue to be a victim of the games men play.

After all, it is your right to be informed.

$14.95   193 pgs   6x9 Paperback   ISBN: 978-0-9840456-4-8